LADY
PREACHERS

FANNING THE
FLAMES OF REVIVAL

LADY PREACHERS

FANNING THE FLAMES OF REVIVAL

BY PAMELA BOLTON

LADY PREACHERS

FANNING THE FLAMES OF REVIVAL

CONTENTS

DEDICATION

This book is dedicated to all the women pastors, evangelists, and revivalists who are passionate about Jesus and who are wholeheartedly serving God throughout the world today.

I especially want to thank Donna Schambach for her kindness and support. She is a powerful woman evangelist who is making a huge difference on the planet, right now, in our day, for the Kingdom of God. What a good example of a Godly woman!

FOREWORD

Sheridan Race II, Ticonderoga Assembly of God, Ticonderoga, NY

Recently, a friend of mine, Rev. Pamela Bolton, told me that she was writing a new book, and later, she asked me to review it. At least initially, I didn't know that I would be selected to write the Foreword. The title is *Lady Preachers: Fanning the Flames of Revival*. Its focus is on tracing the historical accounts of what God accomplished through mighty women of faith, within The United States, between approximately 100 and 170 years ago.

This is an important study, because God is looking for people in every generation who will simply say, "yes," to His call on their lives. In saying "people," this refers to both men and women who are willing to go and serve Him wherever He may call them to. The servant of God is one who is called by Him and is graced with a spiritual gift or gift mix appropriate for the task that He is asking them to do. (For example: A carpenter needs a hammer.) Many people believe that the revivals that have occurred over the past 150 years are a fulfillment of the prophecy of Joel 2:28-29; "And it shall come to pass afterward, that I will pour out my Spirit upon all flesh; and your sons and daughters shall prophesy, your old men shall dream dreams, your young men shall see visions: And also upon the handmaidens in those days will I pour out my Spirit." (NKJV) These verses indicate that God desires for women as well as men to operate in these areas of ministry. In the Old Testament, we find examples of female leadership in the lives of Miriam, a prophetess or prophet; Deborah, both a prophet and a judge; and Huldah, a prophet in the time of Josiah. In the New Testament, Tabitha (Dorcas) had a benevolence ministry (Acts 9:36-43), and Philip's four unmarried daughters were recognized as prophets (Acts 21:8-9). Paul mentions Euodia and Syntyche in the same category as Clement and the rest of his fellow workers (Philippians 4:2-3). Priscilla and her husband, Aquila, ran a house church type of ministry (Acts 18). Pheobe is referred to as a deacon in Acts 16. I could go on and on, but the point is that there are many examples throughout the Bible of women in ministry roles, which far outnumber the few instances where the Bible seems to restrict their involvement, which I will not be commenting on here.

In addition to within Scripture, we have examples from history of women of faith ministering for God, like Maria Woodworth-Etter, Aimee Semple McPherson, Alice Reynolds Flower, Anna Ziese, and Marie Burgess Brown. The feeling you get as you read through this work is this: If God could do it with them in their day, then He can do it with you in your day. When you read their stories, you are actually hearing testimonies of real-life scenarios where God intervened and revival resulted. The power of hearing testimonies like these is that they can cause your faith or your ability to believe it can happen in your life or situation to come alive today.

I have known Pastor Pamela for over ten years as a church member, fellow minister, and friend. I know that it is her desire to see people experience revival in our day. She begins by showing you how for many years in the past, using far less technology than we have today, certain individuals whose hearts were hungry for more of God impacted person after person with a greater hunger for more of Him. This is to cause you to believe that God will do it again, but even more than that, that you would understand that He desires to use you personally in the process. A great definition of "revival" that I once heard was this:

"Light yourself on fire with passion and people will come from miles to watch you burn." Author Unknown

Prepare yourself as you begin to read this book to answer this question: Do I consider myself hungry for more of God at this present moment?

1. If the answer is "no," then, why not?
2. If the answer is "yes," then, what will you do about it?

I sincerely hope you enjoy reading this book and that you consider the impact that these accounts made in the past on many lives as well as the impact they can make on you.

INTRODUCTION

For thousands of years, God has used ladies to help accomplish His will on this planet. Women have played vital roles in laying Godly spiritual foundations throughout the world. The fruit of their labor is the proof; signs, wonders, and miracles followed their preaching and teaching.

Deborah is just one example of a woman, whose story is recounted in the Old Testament, who God used to accomplish His purposes for His people. She operated as a judge, military leader, and prophet; and she is the only judge of Israel who functioned in all three of these roles (Judges 4 & 5). God has and always will use whomever He desires, as long as they are willing to be faithful to Him and participate in His plans.

There are also many well-known mothers of the faith who were used by God in past times of revival and awakening, and we can be encouraged by their stories. Some of them include Harriet Tubman, Maria Woodworth-Etter, Jennie Smith, Amy Semple McPherson, Katherine Khulman, and Mama Mary Jenkins.

My prayer is that as you read these accounts of lady preachers, evangelists, and revivalists, you will be inspired to believe God for what He wants to do through you—right here, right now. If He did something in the past, He'll do it again and even greater, too—if we'll just trust Him. The sky is the limit. Only believe!

It is my heart's desire to see God move in power in our day. I know that He wants to use women, as well as men, in these last days of revival and awakening. It is His will for people to be SAVED (Knowing who they are in Christ), DELIVERED (Completely set free), AND HEALED (Walking in complete health)! Do you want to see God's Kingdom come and His will be done here on Earth, as it is in Heaven? Precious Child of God, I'm confident that God has you here on this planet for… SUCH A TIME AS THIS!

In this book, I am going to focus primarily on mighty women of God who served within the United States, approximately 150 years ago. We can be encouraged by the accounts of their lives, to look ahead to what God wants to do right now, as well as in the future.

OUR GOD IS A RECORD KEEPING GOD!

Ladies, we can sit on the sidelines and watch others fulfill their God-given calls, or we can become active in fulfilling our own. God won't force us. We can still know Him and go to Heaven, but we can miss our call on this planet.

The choice is up to us…. I pray that we will each choose well!

PLEASE NOTE: Any time that you see text in italics in Chapters 1-8, it is my writing. All other text in these chapters is directly quoted from newspaper articles, which are then cited at the end of each section of print. Some minor grammatical and spelling errors were corrected from the original newspapers, for clarity. When you see "???," this indicates places where the newspaper print is illegible.

CHAPTER 1

MEET MISS JENNY SMITH: THE RAILROAD EVANGELIST

Miss Jenny Smith was an invalid as a result of an accident when she was young. She made several trips by train for medical consultations, while on a cot in a baggage car. On one of her journeys, she received a healing in her body when a baggage master prayed with her. As a result, Miss Jenny Smith dedicated her life to sharing the Gospel with the men who worked the railroads.

Who would have thought that God would choose to use a woman to reach the men who worked on the early railroads throughout the United States? God often uses the most unlikely candidates. He can use anyone whom He chooses to, including you.

LADY PREACHER PASSES THROUGH

Jennie Smith, the railroad evangelist, passed through here Tuesday on No. 4 over the B. and O. for the East. She has for years been doing a great work among the railroad men, which has earned her the title of "railroad evangelist." She is known to every railroader and has been the instrument for great good among this class of men.

(**The Clarksburg Telegram.**, May 17, 1901, Image 1)

MISS JENNIE SMITH'S WORK

The annual outing of the Baltimore and Ohio branch of the Young Men's Christian Association, which has been discontinued during the past two years, will be resumed this season and will take place at Island Park, Harpers Ferry, Thursday, July 29....

Miss Jennie Smith, who will make the principal address of the occasion, began a series of noonday meetings this week for the Baltimore and Ohio shop men and trainmen, and during these services extends a personal invitation to the railroad men and their families to be present on the outing. Miss Smith, who is known from coast to coast as the "apostle of the railroad men," is personally acquainted with nearly every man on the Baltimore and Ohio—trainmen as well as office employees. The circumstances leading to her lifelong work of spreading the Gospel among the railroaders being especially interesting.

When a young girl in her teens (she is now past fifty) was an invalid confined to bed, and her parents, being people of means, did all in their power to afford her surgical aid. In visiting specialists in various parts of the country, she made several railroad journeys on a stretcher in the baggage car, and while on one of these trips became engaged in conversation with the baggage master, who suggested the efficacy of prayer as a cure. Jennie Smith and the railroad man prayed together, and she made a vow that, if cured, she would devote her whole life to religious work. Afterward, regaining the use of her limbs, she immediately began work among the railroad men, especially the trainman who is too busy running the train to attend church. For a number of years, she conducted these noonday meetings in shops, roadhouses, etc., assisting many a railroad man to promotion he otherwise could not have obtained. Jennie Smith has been one of the foremost advocates of temperance, and clean living among the trainmen and has accomplished wonderful results in this direction. Conductors and engineers running some of the fastest trains in the country, were converted through her influence when callboys in the roadhouses and messengers ???. No matter what road she travels on, the probabilities are that one of "her boys" is a member of the crew.

(Evening Star., June 26, 1909, Page 8, Image 28)

JENNIE SMITH, RAILWAY VIGIL

In the ranks of this Christian army that invaded Omaha was one little woman who has shaken hands with more railroad men than any other woman in America; she is known to every engineer, fireman, and conductor on the entire network of American railroads. For over thirty years, she has worked among the railroad men; for over twenty years, she lay prone upon a stretcher and traveled in the baggage coach ahead, but she never let up in her great work. The train men protected her and gave her every comfort within their power. She has no use for money—unless it be to help someone less fortunate than she—and she never needs a railway ticket.

The woman is Jennie Smith—a plain, homely name, but of wonderful significance to the railroader. She is the national railroad evangelist of the Women's Christian Temperance Union. But she is more to the men of the railroad. She is the "white light ahead" to the grimy engineer, the dirty fireman, and the immaculate conductor. She is their Jennie *of* Arc, the Eva Booth among the workingmen, the Florence Nightingale to the injured.

Twenty years ago, Jennie Smith addressed the employees of the Union Pacific Railway at the Boyd Theater. Wednesday noon, during the lunch, she went down to the Union Pacific shops and talked to the men. She was not a stranger there, for they had all seen her or heard of her.

One of the first men to greet Jennie Smith upon her arrival in Omaha was a leading business man. The man is E. G. Hampton of the Hampton Lumber Company. Thirty-five years ago, Mr. Hampton, then a tender youth, used to wheel Jennie Smith—crippled Jennie—about in her wheel chair. She was an invalid then, but today, she is well and strong. Can those two ever forget one another?

Another Omaha man to greet Jennie Smith upon her arrival at the Rome Hotel was J. T. Brilliant of the Independent Telephone Company.

"God bless him," said Miss Smith afterward. "I'll never forget him. Twenty years ago, he signed the pledge before me; and I know that pledge has never been broken."
(Omaha Daily Bee., October 31, 1909, HALF-TONE, Image 19)

ANNUAL REUNION OF EMPLOYEES OF B. & O.

WILL BE HELD AT HARPER'S FERRY, WITH MISS JENNIE SMITH, THE "RAILROAD EVENGELIST," IN CHARGE

Miss Jennie Smith, who recently conducted a revival at Zane Street M. E. Church, this city, and her "railroad boys" of the Baltimore and Ohio system are to hold their 30th annual reunion at Island Park, Harper's Ferry, on Thursday, July 27th. The employee's committee in charge

announced that arrangements have been made for the largest gathering of railroad men that ever met at Harper's Ferry, and it is expected that the attendance will exceed 6,000. Special trains will be run by the Baltimore and Ohio from all parts of the system within a day's ride of Harper's Ferry to carry the railroad men and their families to the reunion....

Miss Jennie Smith will make the address of welcome to the railroad men, which will be followed by remarks from several other prominent speakers, including James M. Rice, former secretary Riverside branch of the Baltimore....

Miss Smith's annual reunion is unique to the Baltimore and Ohio System, and the railroad men look forward to it with unusual interest. Jennie Smith is known in railroad circles throughout the United States as the "Little Mother of the Railroad men," and in her mission of carrying the Gospel into the roadhouses, rest houses, telegraph towers, shops and other places of employment, she has made many acquaintances among the erring of the Baltimore and Ohio men. *The first meeting* was held in the summer of 1881, at the Harper's Ferry, and each succeeding year, she has brought them together in a renewal of friendship. A feature of the reunion this year will be the presence of many veteran employees who attended the first meeting in 1881 and are now on *the* retired list.

Miss Smith's evangelistic work among the railroad men was begun on the B. and O. as a young girl, and she stated recently that whenever one sees "B. and O." under the window of a locomotive cab, she feels more at home than at any other time. Made an invalid in childhood as a result of an accident, Miss Smith spent several years bedfast, with no improvement in her condition. Specialists were consulted in various parts of the country from time to time, and while making one of these journeys in a B. & O. baggage car on a cot, the gray-haired baggage master suggested to the young girl that she might find relief through prayer. Miss Smith prayed with the railroad man in the baggage car, promising to devote her lifework, if restored to the use of her limbs, *to* spiritual work among the railroad men. For nearly forty years, she has been fulfilling her promise. (**The Fairmont West Virginian., July 13, 1911, Page 6, Image 7**)

MEETS HER "BOYS" AT PICNIC

Miss Jennie Smith, Railroad Evangelist, Features Annual Gathering

Hundreds of railroad men who have been led to follow the teachings of Christ through the revival meetings of Miss Jennie Smith, railroad evangelist of this city, are to gather at Island Park, Harpers Ferry, WV, tomorrow for their annual picnic. Miss Smith plans to leave on an early morning train for Harpers Ferry, and said today she is expecting a large attendance for "my boys" at the gathering.

For years past, Miss Smith has been laboring among the railroad men from Philadelphia to Grafton, WV, and during the course of her evangelistic meetings over 1,200 have professed conversion. The idea of Miss Smith's "converts" gathering for an annual picnic originated some years ago, and since that time, hundreds have gathered at Harpers Ferry each year.

(**Evening Star., July 30, 1913, Page 10, Image 10**)

CHAPTER 2

LADY PREACHERS, EVANGELISTS, AND REVIVALISTS

During the mid to late 1800s and early 1900s, throughout the United States, there were many women who accepted the call of God on their lives and became preachers, evangelists, and revivalists. The following articles mention just a few who plowed the ground ahead of this generation. They ministered in many different denominations including the Lutheran, Presbyterian, Methodist Episcopal, Baptist, Christian, Free Methodist, Salvation Army, Quaker, Holiness, Congregational, and Methodist Churches. I am sure that there were many others as well. These are just the ones that I happened to discover in my research.

WOMAN AND HOME

A WOMAN PREACHER'S REMARKABLE RECORD

The **Rev. Mary Munns**, Dawson, Spring County, KY, though a woman of limited education, has been licensed as a preacher by a theological college of that state and is by her eloquence and surprising works creating a sensation in the southwest. **She declares that although after her conversion in 1869, she was strongly urged by the inward spirit to preach the Gospel, diffidence in her powers caused her to refuse, whereupon, as a punishment, God deprived her of the use of her hands and feet.**

When this affliction fell upon her, she prayed in these words:

"O Lord, if it is thy will that I should take to the pulpit for the conversion of sinners, restore me the use of my limbs as a confirmatory sign."

This was at night, and the next morning when she arose from her bed, she did so without assistance. Not only that, but she fully possessed the power of her hands and feet, and, as it seemed to her, found an eloquence on her tongue she had never known before. Since she entered the pulpit, she has preached 2,373 sermons and been instrumental in the conversion of thousands of sinners. She does not claim to work miracles, but followers and admirers assert that the laying on of her hands possesses great power of healing.

Mrs. Munns was born in 1852 in Kentucky. It may be said that she is descended from a race of pastors and is the Sam Small among women preachers.—*Chicago Record*
(The Item., February 17, 1898, Page 3, Image 3)

The **Rev. Mrs. Van Cott**, the licensed preacher of the Methodist Episcopal Church has just closed an engagement of two weeks in the church at Springfield, MA, where the local paper reports **"large meetings and fifty conversions,"** and pronounces the lady **"a good preacher and an admirable person to conduct prayer meetings with."**

(The Evening Post., January 08, 1870, Page 1, Image 1)

RELIGIOUS INTELLIGENCE
AND CHURCH ITEMS

...*The St. Louis Christian Advocate*, Methodist, gallantly styles **Mrs. Van Cott** as vain, egotistical, pompous, dogmatic, and bold, besides being given to slang phrases. It says further, **"Mrs. Van Cott was the first regularly licensed lady preacher in the Methodist Episcopal Church, and we respectfully suggest that unless the material be of a different kind and greatly superior, she should be the last."**
(The Catskill Recorder., January 16, 1874, Page 3, Image 3)

A FEMALE REVIVALIST

THE LATEST BALTIMORE SENSATION

W. B. Read, of the *Kingston East Tennessean*, gives the following notice of Mrs. Van Cott, the lady revivalist, who has recently created so much excitement in Baltimore:

The latest sensation here is the preaching of **Mrs. Van Cott, a celebrated revivalist**, who for the past fortnight has been preaching to audiences second only we should judge to those of Beecher at the St. John's M. E. Church on Liberty Street. We went to hear her this morning. Going early, we secured a good seat from which to take observations and hear all she had to say. By eleven o'clock, the hour for beginning services, the large building was literally jammed, when Mrs. Van Cott walked up the aisle and took her seat in the pulpit. She is a portly, apparently well-preserved lady of about forty-five or fifty years of age, quite fleshy, with a pleasant, benignant countenance. Dressed in a plain alpaca, with plain linen collar

and cuffs, and without further ornament than a little gold watch, and a plain black belt round the waist, which secured it. She is a forcible, earnest, and effective speaker; and frequently, during her discourse, had the congregation in tears. Her voice is powerful and could be distinctly heard in any portion of the capacious building. It is also musical and pleasant. Her gestures are also very fine and graceful. **It is said that such an awakening as she has made has not been experienced in St. John's Church for many years. We do not now remember the number of converts made here through her ministrations, but it is very large.**
(Public Ledger., December 05, 1874, Image 1)

AROUND HOME

Mrs. Van Cott, the lady revivalist, is announced to hold forth in Haverstraw this week.
(Rockland County Journal., March 31, 1877, Page 5, Image 5)

Mrs. Van Cott, the woman revivalist who has a wide fame in her line of business, has been engaged and will commence her evangelical efforts about February.
(The Corrector., January 26, 1884, Page 3, Image 3)

RELIGIOUS INTELLIGENCE
AND CHURCH ITEMS

…**"The Hallelujah Lasses"** or **"Salvation Army,"** a **body of lady preachers** under the command of Rev. W. Booth, a well-known clergyman, have been creating some excitement in the North of England.
(The Catskill Recorder., December 13, 1878, Page 3, Image 3)

BROADWAY M. E. CHURCH

SERMON BY A COLORED LADY

An interesting series of revival meetings has been in progress at the Broadway M. E. Church during a period of five weeks. The pastor, Rev. R. P. Christopher, feels gratified in the knowledge that these extra services have been fruitful in the conversion of thirty or more souls, the majority of whom have attached themselves to the society.

Last evening, the exercises were conducted by Mrs. Amanda Smith, a gifted colored woman, who extemporized to the manifest interest of the large congregation assembled in the church. Her remarks, to a large extent devoted to her own experience in being converted, were varied at intervals with singing, in which she ??? off. **When God blessed and gave her a new heart, she said she could not have been more surprised if she had turned white. The change had been radical and thorough, and she got religion through and through.** Frequently, during her narration, the old-fashioned responses, such as "Glory to God" and "Bless the Lord," were uttered by many of the more devoted, in their exuberance of feeling; and this evidently encouraged the speaker. Mrs. Smith remarked relative to shouting that it was rather out of fashion now, even for Methodists; and she was pleased to know that it had not died out here. In that respect, this was the warmest meeting she had attended for a long time. It was a noticeable fact that Mrs. Smith has

FEW OF THE PECULIARITIES

of her race in addressing an audience except in the way of gesture. She has the gift of language and expression of ideas clearly, coupled with a homely, yet forcible, style of illustration. One instance of that head will suffice. When speaking of her condition of mind, just preceding her conversation, she said she then had no more idea as to what she should do or say than (with a momentary hesitation) a stove or one of the lamps fastened to the side walls. At that period, she was uneducated, a servant with a Pennsylvania family, who were very upright and solemn people, but they nor anyone else had ever broached the subject of religion.

The services last night concluded with a prayer meeting, (during ???) the pendency of which nearly a score went forward and knelt at the altar to be prayed with.
(The Brooklyn Daily Eagle., February 08, 1875, Page 2)

WOMAN PREACHER IN ENGLISH TOWN

The little English town of Sunningdale is thoroughly up to date, for it now has a woman as sole minister of its **Congregational Church**. She is **Miss Norah Thompson, who has made a name for herself as an excellent preacher**. She has officiated at marriages, baptisms, and funerals, and is fully qualified for every duty.
(Chateaugay Record and Franklin County Democrat., February 02, 1923, Page 6, Image 6)

The **tent meetings** are arousing considerable interest, and crowds assemble in the tent every night to hear the **lady preacher**.
(The Brunswick Times., December 16, 1897, Image 3)

A LADY PREACHER

Rev. Anna Jackson preached in the **Baptist Church** last Sunday. **A lady preacher is a novelty in these parts, but her sermons were so acceptable and withal, so helpful that it is the wish of all who were present that she may be engaged as regular pastor.**
(**The Massena Observer., May 10, 1900, Page 1, Image 1**)

———◆———

The **Free Methodist Church** of Liberty Falls is blessed this year with a lady preacher. Her name is **Haverlin**.
(**Sullivan County Record., April 20, 1888, Image 5**)

———◆———

JENNIE KING, SOUL SAVER

A Woman Revivalist Who Has Met Great Success in Georgia and South Carolina

Saving souls is the work Mrs. Jennie King believes she has been called to do, and she is doing it in a very successful manner. Many women are anxious to enter public life, but Mrs. King shrank from it, fought against it, and resisted the "call" for years. She is a comely young woman of 28 and was born in Kentucky, but has long been a resident of Dry Valley, GA. As a mere child, she was locally noted for her piety, and at the age of 10 joined the Congregational Church. Her father was very poor, but she managed to secure a fair education by attending the country schools and by hard study at home.

When she was 15, a very stirring revival was held at the Gum Spring Schoolhouse, and Jennie astonished friends and strangers alike by the fervor of her prayers. Two women revivalists were so struck by her religious eloquence that they urged her to begin preaching, but her father was

one of those old-fashioned men who believe woman's sphere is the home; and she shrank from entering the pulpit. She even married, hoping that the "still, small voice" within her would be silenced, but marriage, maternity even, did not bring about the desired result. Finally, she told her husband that she felt irresistibly impelled to save souls. At first, he strongly objected to the idea, but he now declares that her course is the only one she could conscientiously pursue. **Her revival work has thus far been confined to Georgia and South Carolina, but her great success in securing conversions has caused her to receive cordial invitations from other neighboring states. She is almost constantly engaged in reading the Bible, and she reads nothing else, not even a newspaper.**
(**Evening Capital., November 11, 1895, Image 3**)

WOMAN PREACHER

The **Rev. Mrs. Blanch Blake, leading negro woman preacher of America, begins a revival at Scott Chapel M. E. Church Cedar and Mesa Avenues** Sunday at 11 o'clock. Rev. Blake is a stirring singer and strong preacher. Rev. G. W. Walron, pastor, is planning to make this meeting one of the strongest spiritual drives ever held in the city. **None will be disappointed who attend these services.**
(**Pueblo Chieftain., November 11, 1921, Page 12, Image 12**)

THE GIRL PREACHER

Mrs. Marguerite Isabelle Rice, the independent evangelist and well-known and original girl preacher, will be in Warren to hold a series of meetings in a short time. **Mrs. Rice is only 28 years of age, but has spoken to more people during the past 14 years than any other evangelist or public speaker in America, having made a specialty of prison and**

street work, visiting every state in the union, and preaching in all the principal cities, often tilling return engagements, speaking in the largest churches, opera houses, halls, and upon the streets. Also having the honor *of* being the only preacher holding special permits from Mayors Strong, Low, and McClelland, of New York City, to preach on Broadway.
(Warren Sheaf., September 13, 1906, Image 1)

A LADY PREACHER

Hyde Park boasts of a **lady preacher. Mrs. J. H. Inman** occupies the pulpit of the **M. E. Church**, of which her husband, Rev. J. H. Inman is pastor, every third Sunday evening of the month. Rev. Inman has a double charge, which includes the M. E. Church at Staatsburg, where he preaches on the evenings that his wife is giving interesting sermons at Hyde Park.
(Poughkeepsie Eagle., July 22, 1904, Page 8, Image 8)

MADRID

Mrs. M. L. Jackson, of Springfield, MA, was invited to spend a couple of Sabbaths with the **Baptist Church** of this place, with a view of securing her services as pastor. She preached for us on May 6. On the evening of May 13, the church voted unanimously, to extend to her a call to become their pastor. Mrs. Jackson did not give her decision until Sunday, May 20. She is accustomed to much larger fields and a stronger church, but having only recently recovered from nervous prostration, she felt that her strength was not sufficient to do the work in a large field, although she has had some flattering calls. On the evening of May 20, she accepted the call to this church. We had feared that she would not accept and are indeed gratified that she has consented to do so, and the church will

look forward with renewed hope and courage. **A lady pastor may be an innovation in this section, but in many parts of the country, it is nothing new, especially in Massachusetts, where Mrs. Jackson came from. One prominent clergyman writes: "All women are not called into the work of preaching the Gospel, but some women have been called in all ages. Mrs. Jackson has been signally called of God to this work, and few men possess the talent and ability of this lady preacher and pastor."** I append below a passage from a long article written of her by Rev. R. S. McArthur, D.D., of New York. He says: "Modesty, propriety, ability, and consecration mark her life and labors wherever she goes. Churches served by Mrs. Jackson will have faithful, conscientious service; and she will give wise and judicious management. He is a bold man who would hinder this goodly woman from doing such godly work." We bespeak the most cordial Christian fellowship for our pastor from all the churches. Wm. OLIN, for Pulpit Com.
(Norwood News., 1878-1941, May 29, 1900, Image 8)

Mrs. M. A. Jackson, a talented lady preacher, has been employed by the **Newark Baptist Church**.
(The Marion Enterprise., May 23, 1896, Page 3, Image 3)

Rev. Anna H. Shaw preached a few days ago in the largest church in Toronto. *The Toronto Globe* says: **"The Methodists of the city showed their appreciation of the lady preacher by crowding the great edifice, even to the remotest corner."**
(Plattsburgh Republican., February 15, 1890, Page 2, Image 2)

Another **lady preacher** has secured a pulpit in Boston. Her name is **Lora Haines**.
(The Dansville Advertiser., February 19, 1874, Page 2, Image 2)

COLORED PEOPLE PLAN REVIVAL

WOMAN PREACHER HERE

The colored people of the city of Keokuk, *IA*, will have revival services to be started on Easter Sunday. **They will be conducted by Mrs. M. E. Wilson, noted negro woman preacher**....

Mrs. Wilson, according to Mr. Butler, "is the greatest and most successful woman preacher and revivalist among the colored people. Her anecdotes from real life are the most graphic and thrilling I have ever heard. She preached here for us a few nights last year, with great results. The people became enamored of her, and the demand for her now is practically unanimous."

(The Daily Gate City and Constitution-Democrat., April 14, 1916, Image 9)

RELIGIOUS

Miss Smiley, the lady preacher who is conducting the services at the **Congregational Church** in this city this week, is meeting with great success. **Her sermons are very fine, eloquent, and interesting. The edifice is crowded every evening, and undoubtedly through Miss Smiley's efforts much good will be accomplished. E. H. S.**

(Evening Courier & Republic., January 07, 1874, Page 1)

Mrs. Thistlethwaite, a lady preacher, is just now the sensation in London. The excitement to hear her continues to increase in fashionable circles, Mrs. Thistlethwaite speaks, dresses, and altogether demeans herself in good taste. A black silk dress, with plain white collar and cuffs, her hair neatly

arranged, an earnest, thoughtful countenance, combined with the evident sincerity of her motives and the dignity of her movements, forbid anything like levity on the part even of a large miscellaneous congregation. She speaks fluently and persuasively, without any note, and with considerable force and elegance. At times her attitudes, her outstretched arms command rapt attention.
(Lansingburgh Weekly Chronicle., June 06, 1865, Page 1)

LADY PREACHER DRAWS CROWD

Record Breaking Audience Turns Out at Swedish Lutheran Church on East Side

The audience at the Swedish Lutheran Church of the East Side yesterday was a record breaker owing to the previous announcement that had been made that Mrs. A. W. Stark of DeKalb, would address the congregation instead of the pastor, Frank Haagland, delivering the regular sermon.

Mrs. Stark spoke on charity work, and especially on orphan homes, using the situation on Jollet as an instance.
(The Lake County Times., October 21, 1907, EVENING EDITION, Page 5, Image 5)

YANKTON NOTES

The **revival meeting** which was held at Mr. Loveli's closed last Sunday night. The meeting was conducted by a **lady preacher from Portland**. There was much interest manifested in the meeting.
(The Oregon Mist., May 13, 1910, Image 2)

CAROLINE E. TALBOTT DEAD

Special Dispatch to the Intelligencer

STEUBENVILLE, OH

Jan. 11—**Caroline E. Talbott, the leading lady preacher for the Society of Friends** at their yearly meetings and known all over the United States, died today at her home in Mt. Pleasant. Age 64 years. She had been preaching for thirty years in her adopted church.

(The Wheeling Daily Intelligencer., January 12, 1894, Page 4)

Miss Stevens, a beautiful blonde lady preacher, is creating a profound religious sensation in Georgia. She is said to make all the masculines feel like embracing Christianity, or at least its exponent and advocate.

(Helena Weekly Herald., May 23, 1872, Page 4, Image 4)

LOCAL NEWS

The **Holiness meeting** at Kelly's Chapel began on Thursday night of last week and will continue for 10 days. The meeting is being conducted by Elders Johnson and Smith, of Cottage Mound, MO, and **a lady preacher** from Arkansas.

(The Covington Leader., August 01, 1918, Page 2, Image 2)

"MORE MATTERS FOR A MAY MORNING"

Mrs. Harrod, the sensational lady preacher, has been here eighteen days up to this evening. She began her sanctification series Thursday, April 25th, and has held an almost continuous service, afternoons and evenings, sometimes lasting until 2 o'clock AM. It is a matter of considerable comment that she has several men, women, and boys under "conviction." This is denoted by lachrymose languor (*tearful feeling*) in the church and by their behavior on the street. Holding heads down, shuffling feet, sighing, and groaning, forsooth! One of those under "conviction" acknowledged a debt of two cents to a local grocer in his testimony. Another is in a state of partial collapse, owing to overwrought feeling. Another weeps copiously and shakes his head as he walks along the street. Another asks as she walks sanctimoniously up and down the aisles of the church, "Are ye goin' to get dipped, hey?" It was a misstatement that both of her children are dead, one of them, a boy, is now in his father's custody. One of Mrs. Harrod's sanctified assistants told a young lady who had not chosen to approach the "mourners bench" at her beck and call, that her father who had recently died was in Hell, too! This prophesier of future events is respectfully referred to the ninth commandment. Mrs. Harrod in her frenzy, ordered fire from Heaven last Saturday evening to scorch the unbelieving sinners present. It was not forthcoming! Further advices from Mt. Carmel are to this effect. That she laid on the floor of the church during one of her meetings, thumping it with her heels and making such a noise that one of the sisters present, a good friend of hers, thinking to lessen the strain upon her lower extremities, folded up a piece of carpet and placed it under her feet. When she found out it was there, she very ceremoniously kicked it to one side. The consensus of public opinion here regarding these meetings is that the sermons are good enough, "whose words took all ears captive," if shorn of the acrobatic, terpsichorean, and trance accessories. **And the writer begs leave to state that, in referring to these proceedings, he is not and has no**

intention of making a mockery of true religion, but in asserting his privilege of giving the news concerning any occurrences odd or strange. And surely these are both odd and strange.

(The Evening Bulletin., May 14, 1901, Image 4)

LADY PREACHER AT POUNDING MILL HOLDS PROTRACTED MEETINGS AT WHICH ARE MANY CONVERSIONS

Mrs. Nannie B. Osborne preached here Sunday at 11 o'clock, and in the afternoon returned to Honaker, where she preached in the street at 7 o'clock to about 500 people. The people came in wagons, hacks, buggies, and automobiles. The meeting at the church that night lasted until 11 o'clock in spite of the fact that it was dismissed three times. During her part of the two weeks meeting, between twenty and thirty conversions are reported, besides a large number of back-sliders, renewed their covenant with God. All the ministers of the town were present the last night; *there* were six additions to the Baptist Church, four to the Methodist, and two to the M. E. South. She spoke of the kind people in glowing terms of praise for their hospitality. She held the meeting for Rev. A. N. Conner, the pastor of the M. E. Church. Mr. James Osborne, father-in-law of Mrs. Osborne, attended the meetings Sunday night at Honaker, and said he never saw anything like it—such an interest—and on Monday accompanied Mrs. Osborne to her home in Princeton for a visit.

(Clinch Valley News., July 10, 1914, Image 1)

A lady preacher now fills the pulpit of the **Franklinville Baptist Church**.

(The Brockport Republic., July 14, 1881, Page 3, Image 3)

Rev. Mrs. **David Jones** of West Exeter will preach here at the **Baptist Church** Sunday afternoon at the usual hour of services. All are cordially invited to come and hear the lady preacher.

(The Freeman's Journal and the Oneonta Press., June 14, 1922, Page 7, Image 7)

A LADY PREACHER

We learn that **Miss Mary Susan Little** preached in Eckhart Baptist Church Sunday, 17th inst., **to a large and attentive audience**. "The sermon was a well-directed effort and highly appreciated by all present. This pious lady has just returned from Kansas. She spent several years in Eckhart prior to the war engaged in teaching school. As an instructor of youth, she has been very successful and never failing in making strong impressions. Her many friends are pleased to meet her and hope that her useful life may be long continued."

(Frostburg Mining Journal., November 23, 1878, Image 3)

LEWISTON, NORTH IDAHO

Rev. Mrs. **Barrows, a very eloquent lady preacher**, will occupy the **Christian Church** pulpit next Sunday.

(Lewiston Teller., December 31, 1898, Image 3)

BRIDGEPORT, CT

WOMAN OCCUPIED PULPIT OF CHURCH AT PORT

PORT CHESTER, NY

Sept. 13—On Sunday, for the first time in the history of the King Street Methodist Church, a woman preacher occupied the pulpit. She was Mrs. Charles Pittman, wife of the pastor of the church. She was filling her husband's position, because he had been suddenly called to England, to the bedside of his dying mother.

Although it was not until the latter part of the week that the announcement was made that Mrs. Pittman, and not Mr. Pittman, would preach on Sunday. The news was quickly passed around, and as a result, the cozy little church contained a large congregation on Sunday morning. In fact, it was the largest congregation that has been present in some time. There were about five women to every man, and among those present were many school teachers. Many people outside of those who regularly attend came to hear the woman preacher, and there were Port Chester people among them. Many of the people came quite early, as though they wished to miss nothing. It may have been curiosity that brought some, but with the congregation made up mostly of women, it appeared that the members of the gentle sex had come to hear one of their number, because it is not often that they can sit and listen to a woman preach from a pulpit. But Mrs. Pittman was in no way affected by the large congregation before her, and from the time she announced the first hymn until she recited the benediction, the service was carried out without a hitch.

In no way did the work of preaching seem to effect Mrs. Pittman. She wore a cream colored gown with short sleeves and a square cut neck, and her hair was done up in a knot effect and rather low on the head. Her pronounced English accent magnetically held the attention of everyone in the assemblage, from the opening to the close of the service. At times, the preacher waxed eloquent as she became enthused with her theme, and emphatic gestures added force to her statements.

As Mrs. Pittman was about to open the service, someone placed a bouquet of roses on the communion table. The lady preacher stepped into the choir loft and borrowed a watch from one of the male singers, in order that she might not preach too long.

She opened the program of morning worship by announcing the hymn, "Oh, for a Thousand Tongues." When the hymn had been sung, the regular order of service was continued. For the lesson, the preacher read the twenty-second chapter of Genesis and commented on the verses as she read.

When she had finished, she briefly announced the reason for her being in the pulpit. **She said that there was a great work for the person in the pew as well as for the person in the pulpit.** She appealed to the congregation and particularly to the members of the church to do all that they could towards making the work go along smoothly during the pastor's absence, and towards making it fruitful.

Mrs. Pittman preached for half an hour. She said, among other things, that sermons would be more effective if those in the pews would pursue the old custom of following the lesson with their own Bibles. She lamented the fact that this custom has become a thing of the past, and also told of the benefits derived from taking notes from the sermons. Continuing with her theme, the preacher said that she liked to see young people have a good time, She said that she did not believe in straight-backed religion, which many people thought essential to their being saved, but she warned the young people against forgetting God. "Have a good time, but don't leave God out of your calculations," she said. "If you do, you will miss something."

During her discourse, the lady pastor told of the first time she spoke in public. She was at college at the time, she said, and as a member of one of the young women's societies, was one evening called upon to pray. Her heart *felt* faint within her when her name was called, she said, but she managed to struggle along until she finished. After that, she said, it was an easier thing to face an audience.

At the conclusion of the service on Sunday morning, Mrs. Pittman, who, like her husband, is extremely popular throughout the community, was surrounded by the women folks and warmly congratulated. She expressed gladness at being able to take her husband's place. Although ministers from other churches may be procured during a part of the time while Rev. Pittman is away from his church, Mrs. Pittman will occupy the pulpit again probably next Sunday.

(The Bridgeport Evening Farmer., September 13, 1911, Page 5, Image 5)

BARTON COUNTY, KS

MRS. GLAZE HERE NEXT SUNDAY

Mrs. Glaze was over from Pawnee Rock and held services at the **Christian Church,** both morning and evening last Sunday.

Mrs. Glaze is an Australian by birth and spent many years of her life in that country. She left there several years ago, however, and has been an evangelist, traveled over England, the United States, and through many of the uncivilized countries of the old world. She was in San Francisco at the time of the great earthquake and fire. She has preached the Word of God for many years and is a direct, forceful speaker who will captivate your attention; and you will be profoundly interested in her talk next Sunday, when she will again fill the pulpit at the Christian Church, morning and evening.

Don't miss the opportunity of hearing this lady preacher.
(**Barton County Democrat.**, **January 12, 1912, Image 1**)

MEADE, KS

NYE GLEANINGS

Camp meeting will begin at Tainter's Grove next Friday evening with a lady preacher in charge.
(**Meade County News.**, **May 17, 1906, Image 4**)

HARTFORD, KY

THE GREAT REVIVAL

The great revival, which has been in progress at the Cumberland Presbyterian Church for the past three weeks, still continues with increased interest. Many of the worldly have professed religion—some very old men have turned their backs on the world and are entering the straight and narrow way to a better land. **Mrs. Woosley, the lady preacher, has certainly done a work for Hartford that has long been needed, of which others have failed to accomplish.**

Upwards of a hundred have been converted during the meeting and the probabilities are that many more will be saved before the close.

There are a number of people who do not approve of women preaching, but here is an example of woman's work in the pulpit, and it is truly great. Most assuredly, such work as has been done by Mrs. Woosley is a brilliant success and will so be received in Heaven.
(The Hartford Republican., December 21, 1900, Image 3)

———————

Rev. Anna H. Shaw preached a few days ago in the largest church of Toronto. The Methodists of the city showed their appreciation of the lady preacher by crowding the great edifice even to the remotest corner. She held a second meeting, also very largely attended, in the afternoon. At the two services between six and seven thousand persons were present. Miss Shaw had magnificent audiences all through her week's work in Canada.—*The Toronto (Canada) Globe.*

Rev. Anna Shaw is one of the most fluent of speakers, speaking extemporaneously with the glibness of the swiftest reader, gliding from one point to another with marvelous ease and celerity *(fast movement)*, and well-chosen, distinctly enunciated language and holds the audience deeply interested from first to last.—*Hartford (Conn.) Times*

The announcement that the Rev. Anna H. Shaw was to speak before the Woman's Suffrage Association in the hall of the House of Representatives last night had the effect of attracting a large audience. The standing room was all taken and the galleries were filled. Rev. Shaw made a good address: it was logical, instructive, and eloquent.—*Col. (Ohio) Dispatch*
(The Enterprise., November 25, 1891, Page 5, Image 5)

———————

WEDONIA, KY

Several from this neighborhood went to Orangeburg Sunday to hear the **lady preacher** who is attracting great crowds *at* every service.

(The Evening Bulletin., May 08, 1901, Image 4)

KIRKSVILLE, MO

BEYOND THE RIVER

Miss Land, a lady preacher, is the attraction at Baden this week. She has been preaching at various places on this side of the river for some time, and **is attracting immense crowds.** She is a noted singer and revivalist.

(Weekly Graphic., January 04, 1895, Image 3)

OREGON, MO

The meetings under the direction of the **Misses Power and Walker** are still in progress at the **Christian Church** and will continue throughout this week. Considerable interest is being taken and **the lady preacher seems to be able to explain the teachings of the Bible better than the average speaker.**

(The Holt County Sentinel., November 30, 1917, Image 8)

ALMOND, NY

The Sun says Almond has **a lady preacher**, a lady merchant, and a lady barber.

(Bolivar Breeze., 1891-1965, January 18, 1900, Image 1)

CORFU, NY

Caolkens, the lady preacher, gave her congregation a good sermon on Saturday and Sunday evenings. (**The Daily News., February 28, 1882, Page 1, Image 1**)

GALLUPVILLE, NY

Gallupville **M. E. Church** Commencing Monday, Nov. 12th, we are to have with us Rev. and Mrs. Johnson Brogdale of the First M. E. Church, Crescent, NY, who are to lead us in a special two weeks evangelical campaign. **Our friends have been preaching the Gospel of Jesus Christ for upwards of forty years, and are safe, sane, and very interesting.** You ought to make up your mind to come and hear them. Meetings every evening with the exception of Saturday. Mrs. Brogdale, who has long been a wife and mother, and who has a very rich and interesting experience, will conduct two meetings for women only on Wednesday afternoons at 2:00 o'clock. Every woman and girl in the district and out of district is very earnestly requested to attend these special meetings. The evening services are to commence at 7:30. On Sunday, November 19, the pulpit in the morning at ??? will be occupied by Mrs. Brogdale who is well worth hearing. If you have never heard a lady preacher, here is your opportunity. Come and hear Mrs. Brogdale. She has a message for you. She will also preach at West Berne at 2 o'clock in the afternoon.

Special singing will be a feature at all of the meetings, and we want you to come and help us. We shall sing the old-fashioned songs, like mother used to sing. Let us see you joining in.

Pray for us, that God's people may be quickened and that the sinners may be converted. The greatest need in the world today is Christ. Get to know Him, then introduce Him to others. He is the only safe cure for all the world's ills. Any League of Nations, any World Conference, and peace plans that leave Him out, must needs be a failure. He is the world's only hope.

(Altamont Enterprise., November 16, 1923, Page 2, Image 2)

SALEM, OR

GO TO CHURCH SUNDAY

Come and hear the lady preacher at 11 AM and 8 PM. **Mrs. Mary Presnall is an able speaker and one that stands for the old-time religion.** Sunday school at 10 AM. Christian Endeavor at 6:45 PM. Everyone is welcome. Monthly meetings next fifth day at 8 PM.

(Daily Capital Journal., October 06, 1917, News-Autos, Image 9)

WATAGUA, TN

The protracted meeting is still in progress. The lady preacher, Mrs. M. L. Westcoat, has been preaching some excellent sermons, and great crowds have been in attendance. The house will not hold the people who have crowded in from all directions. There have been as many as eighteen at the anxious seat at once, and there have been several professions.

(The Comet., March 14, 1895, Image 1)

ALVARADO, TX

A LADY PREACHER

The largest protracted meeting (*going on for days, weeks, or months*) ever known in the history of this country is now in progress at the Methodist Church, and a novel attraction of the services is a lady preacher. Great crowds flock from the four corners of the earth to hear sanctification, or a second blessing, preached.
(Fort Worth Daily Gazette., August 17, 1886, Image 1)

WOMAN PREACHER ILL

Rev. P. S. Vining, known through the Adirondacks as the woman preacher at the lumber camps, is reported seriously ill of grippe at Saranac Lake. She is an ordained Baptist minister.
(Ticonderoga Sentinel., January 25, 1923, Page 1, Image 1)

I heard a fine sermon yesterday by a lady preacher of the Unitarian faith. I don't like to see women in the pulpit or on the platform, but whether I like it or not they are coming to the front. This preacher lady from Iowa gave us some pure gospel. The people here are a cosmopolitan crowd. Coming from everywhere, of course, they represent every shade of public thought, politics, and theology—and we are tolerant of differences and move along quite harmoniously.
(Times-Promoter., February 18, 1909, Image 4)

WATERTOWN, WI

In its issue of last week, the newspaper at Barneveld, Wisconsin, speaks of a Watertown lady preacher, Mrs. Edward Davis, as follows: **Mrs. Davis, the lady preacher of Watertown**, preached at the **Congregational Church** in this village last Sunday morning and Monday evening to a large and appreciative congregation. Mrs. Davis is an eloquent speaker and her sermons are powerful and convincing. Mrs. Davis was received last summer to the Welsh Congregational Conference as an evangelist and since then has been doing considerable work among the churches of this denomination.

(Watertown Republican., 1860-1906, March 10, 1886, Image 5)

Chapter 3

Lady Preacher Impacts President Lincoln

LINCOLN AND MRS. GURNEY

THE STORY AS TOLD IN A RECENT MEMOIR OF THE QUAKER LADY

An interesting episode, scarcely, if at all, known to the public hitherto, which occurred in the latter years of President Lincoln's life, is described in the forthcoming yearly obituary volume of the Society of Friends, entitled the *Annual Monitor for 1883*. It is related in connection with a memoir of the late Mrs. E. P. Gurney, widow of the well-known Quaker, Mr. Joseph Gurney, of Norwich. On her husband's decease, Mrs. Gurney returned to America, the land of birth, and chiefly resided for the remainder of her life at Burlington, in New Jersey. She was one of the recognized lady preachers of the Society of Friends, and, as such, undertook several missionary journeys. During the terrible civil war, she felt great sympathy for the very difficult and responsible position in which President Lincoln had been placed by the course of events, and she believed it to be her duty to seek an interview with him for the purpose of endeavoring to animate him by religious exhortation and prayer. In company with three of her friends as companions, she proceeded to Washington. What followed is thus described in the memoir in the Annual Monitor, which is written by an English barrister, a Friend, who was intimately acquainted with Mr. J. J. Gurney and herself:

"It was a critical period in the autumn of 1862. The armies of Lee and McClellan were confronting each other in the neighborhood of Washington, and the President, finding the capitol in danger, had issued a call for several hundred thousand additional troops. Every available moment of his time was precious, and two days were spent by Mrs. Gurney and the friends who accompanied her in fruitless efforts to see him. They had given up all hope, when, to use her own words, 'the great iron door' seemed to open of itself, and a most interesting interview we had.' It was on a Sunday morning, in a beating rain, that the little party repaired to the Whitehouse, where they were at once introduced into the private apartment of President Lincoln. They quickly recognized his tall, commanding figure as he rose to receive them, and the cordial grasp of his hand, as they were separately named to him, at once placed them at ease. Deep thoughtfulness and intense anxiety marked his countenance and created involuntary sympathy for him in this great national crisis. He at first supposed Mrs. Gurney to be from England, but was soon undeceived.

"She gave him to understand that it was not motive of idle curiosity which had included her to seek an interview, but that she had come in the love of the Gospel of our Lord and Savior, Jesus Christ, that blessed Gospel which breathes 'Glory to God in the highest; on earth, peace, good will toward men.' She then proceeded to assure him of the deep sympathy which, in common with the other members of the Society of Friends, and, indeed, with every true-hearted citizen of United States, she had felt for the President in his arduous duties. He listened with respectable attention, while she calmly unfolded in an address, the delivery of which occupied about 15 minutes, her religious wishes on his behalf. She then knelt in fervent supplication for him and her country. It was an affecting scene. The little party stood in reverential awe, the President appearing bowed in heart under the weight of his responsibilities. The bright waters of the Potomac were glistening in the distance, upon the shores of which stood, even then, the two opposing armies, arrayed against each other, awaiting the awful moment when they should meet in mortal conflict.

"As Mrs. Gurney was leaving, the President took her hand, and holding it for a few moments in silence, said, in a very deliberate manner, 'I am glad of this interview. In the very responsible situation in which I am placed, as a humble instrument in the hands of my Heavenly Father, I have desired that all my words and actions may be in accordance with His will; but if, after endeavoring to do my best, with the light which He affords me, I find my efforts fail, then I must believe that, for some purpose unknown to me, He wills otherwise. If I had my way, this war would never have been, but nevertheless it came. If I had my way, the war would have ended before this; but nevertheless it continues. We must conclude that He permits it for some wise purpose, though we may not be able to comprehend it. For we cannot but believe that He who made the world still governs it. I repeat that I am glad of this interview.'"

Some time afterward, Mrs. Gurney addressed a letter to President Lincoln, to which, after a considerable interval, he replied as follows:

EXECUTIVE MANSION, WASHINGTON
Sept. 4, 1864

Eliza P. Gurney:

My Esteemed Friend: I have not forgotten, probably never shall forget, the very impressive occasion when yourself and friends visited me, on a Sabbath forenoon, two years ago. Nor has your kind letter, written nearly a year later, ever been forgotten. In all, it has been your purpose to strengthen my reliance on God. I am much indebted to the good Christian people of this country for their constant prayers and consolations, and to no one more than yourself. The purposes of the Almighty are perfect and must prevail, though we, erring mortals, may fail to accurately perceive them in advance.

We hoped for a happy termination of this terrible war long before this, but God knows best and has ruled otherwise. We shall yet acknowledge His wisdom and our own error therein. Meanwhile, we must work earnestly in the best light He gives us, trusting that so working still conduces to the great end He ordains.

Surely, He intends some great good to follow this mighty convulsion, which no mortal could make and no moral could stay. Your people, the Friends, have had and are having a very great trial. On the principle of faith opposed to both war and oppression, they can only practically oppose oppression by war. In the hard dilemma, some have chosen one horn and some the other. For those appealing to me on conscientious grounds, I have done and shall do, the best I could and can in my own conscience and under the oath to the law. That you believe this I doubt not, and, believing it, I shall still receive, for my country and myself, your earnest prayers to our Father in Heaven.

Your Sincere Friend,
A. Lincoln

The memoir continues:

"The course of public events is well known. It is unnecessary here to do more than allude to the fact that soon after the foregoing letter was penned its noble-minded writer was for the second time elected President of the United States. His inauguration took place in March 1865, and within a few weeks from that time, he had the joy of seeing the war brought to a close. He lived but a few days after this great result had been achieved. A pang of astonished grief startled the people of America and of the whole civilized world on hearing the tidings of his assassination. Mrs. Gurney had the mournful satisfaction of learning that her letter to the President, written nearly two years previously, had been carefully treasured up by him and was in his breast pocket when the fatal ball struck him."

(Rockland County Journal., Volume 33, May 5, 1883)

We may never know on this side of Heaven how the seeds that we have planted have taken root and produced fruit... souls that will be with Jesus for all of eternity. Thank God that He brings the increase.

CHAPTER 4

YOUNGEST GIRL PREACHERS

I was very surprised at the number of young female preachers and evangelists who were listed in old newspaper articles. I had no idea that there were so many of them.

FROM NEWPORT, RI

A GIRL PREACHER—PERSONAL ITEMS

The little girl preacher has been the attraction in religious circles for the past few days.

Sunday morning and afternoon, she was at Mt. Olive and spoke to a crowded house. In the evening, **she spoke at Bethel to more than 700 persons**. On Tuesday evening, she spoke at Rev. Gunner's Church, the Union Congregational and on Wednesday at Shiloh Baptist Church also to crowded houses. She is a very bright, interesting child. She is trying to raise funds to educate herself for her work, and she lifted richly deserved collections.

Owing to the fact that the little girl preacher was at the Bethel Church on Sunday evening, the Rev. Byron Gunner postponed the third in his series of illustrated sermons until Sunday evening 23rd.
(Richmond Planet., October 22, 1898, Page 5, Image 5)

A NINE-YEAR-OLD GIRL PREACHER

A phenomenal 9-year-old negro girl preacher has developed at Society Hill, SC. For a week, the child has conducted a series of meetings, and the effect of her preaching is wonderful. She is without education and developed her strange powers not more than ten days ago. At first, she preached only to negros, but now white people are flocking to hear her; and the whole country round about is in great excitement. **She quotes Scripture by the chapter, uses good language, and shows amazing insight into the frailties of humanity. A number of conversions are reported from her work.**

(Fisherman & Farmer., July 26, 1895, Image 1)

YOUNG GIRL EVANGELIST CONVERTS THOUSANDS

San Francisco, Cal—**Uldine Utley, eleven year-old girl evangelist**, conducted her first big meeting in San Francisco. **The child has been preaching for six months and has made thousands of converts.** She is a blue-eyed, golden-haired, a laughing, frolicking youngster, like any other little girl of eleven, and yet from her lips fall such phrases as: **"The main points of my commission are three in number: Salvation, divine healing, and baptism of the Holy Spirit."**

"I firmly believe in the doctrine of immaculate conception—in the virgin birth." "I'm a fundamentalist as opposed to the school of modernists—the latter don't accept every word of Holy Writ, whereas the fundamentalist says each line of the Bible is literally true."

(The Suffolk County News., February 29, 1924, Page 11)

A GIRL PREACHER

The Doncaster (England) **12-year-old girl preacher**, Frances Bradley Storr, who exhibited her extraordinary talent, is fast accumulating a long list of engagements in various parts of the country; and her appearance in London cannot be for some time, owing to numerous calls made upon her.

In one month, she had preached to over 5,000 persons and made 400 converts. She exhibits with *evident* satisfaction a crucifix and other Roman ornaments handed to her by one convert.

Quiet in demeanor and plainly attired, there is nothing about the outwardly to indicate the possession of extraordinary talent. When called upon, Miss Storr was preparing her scripture lesson for school, for since she commenced preaching, she has left the public elementary school at Hexthorpe and attends a private school.

When in the pulpit, she invariably wears a white or cream dress, which emphasizes her olive complexion and makes more pronounced her bright, sparkling eyes. Asked how she began to preach, she replied: "I felt a keen desire to join in the services and kept asking my mother, who is a missioner, to let me join her, until at last, she took me to a service and let me read the lesson and speak on it."

The girl preacher began at Norton, near Dorcaster, last September, and has been taking services regularly ever since. **Her manner is subdued and earnest, and big men, she says, are often brought to tears when listening to her earnest appeals.**

"Do you read any particular books?" she was asked.

"No," she replied, "except the Bible," a great portion of which she knows by heart. Asked how she got her ideas for her sermons, she could not explain, and said: "I simply sit down and write them down and take notes into the pulpit, when the ideas come fast enough."

"Has the preaching been a strain upon you or affected your health?"

She smilingly replied: "Not at all. I am told I grow fat on preaching."

She writes out her sermons in full but goes into the pulpit with a postcard containing the principal heads, trusting to her memory to fill in the details. She preaches somewhere every Sunday night. Her sermons last from twenty-five to forty minutes, and converts result from each service.

(Omaha Daily Bee., August 18, 1907, Page 4, Image 28)

YOUNGEST PREACHER GETS RECORD CROWD SUNDAY

OKMULGEE, OK

Miss Orietta Stoddard, 13-year-old girl preacher, Sunday night preached her first sermon here since she became a licensed preacher. Although the church was packed and standing room was hard to find, the youthful clergy woman did not falter in her talk. After the sermon, she spent time exhorting her hearers to seek a new life, but there were no responses. A number of other youthful converts joined the girl preacher and stood with her while she closed the services. Other churches of the city were almost deserted, and one pastor asked members of the choir and others who desired to hear the young woman to do so.

(The Daily Ardmoreite., March 14, 1922, Page 7, Image 7)

MAKES PULPIT DEBUT
(Part of a larger article)

Miss Stoddard made her pulpit debut in her home town, Miami, where she now is in the seventh grade at school. She first attracted widespread attention as a preacher, however, when she delivered a sermon to the congregation of the First Methodist Church at Baxtor Springs, KS. The Rev. O. B. Morris, District Superintendent, declared she led more young people to the Gospel on that occasion than had the regular minister during any previous meeting.

Two years ago, the girl preacher, after joining the church, began her religious work. Under the direction of her pastor, the Rev. G. A Kleinsteiper, of Miami, she prepared her first sermon, which was delivered from the Rev. Kleinsteiper's pulpit.

Miss Stoddard plans to complete her high school education at Miami and will attend the Oklahoma City Methodist College to finish her Gospel training. During the approaching school vacation, however, she will be assigned regular preaching.

(The Washington Times., March 02, 1922, LATE FINANCIAL, Page 6, Image 6)

GIRL PREACHER WINS FAME

CHILD WHO "DIED AND CAME BACK" SEEMS SUDDENLY INSPIRED

Mary McCain, 13, of Longview, MS, a **girl evangelist**, is leaping into fame all over the south as the child preacher who "died, went to heaven, and came back."

Physicians shake their heads when told that Mary died and came back, but her parents are emphatic that Mary was dead. She had no pulse, her heart was not beating, and her body was cold and rigid, they declare.

The following morning, when her body was to be embalmed, Mary McCain came "back to life" when her grief-stricken parents entered the room.

The remarkable thing about the young missioner is that Mary had never been to Sunday School, never saw a Bible, and seldom heard the name of God except in a curse.
(The Glasgow Courier., November 26, 1915, Page 12, Image 12)

15 YEAR OLD GIRL PREACHER

The **15-year-old daughter of Rev. O. E. Croft, who is the pastor of the Baptist churches at Salisbury Corners and Stratford, is creating something of a mild sensation as a preacher.** The young woman recently occupied the pulpits of the Baptist churches at Stratford and Salisbury in place of her father and gave discourses that were pronounced by all who heard them to be logical and well presented, showing careful thought and preparation. The two congregations voted an opinion in favor of a preacher's license being issued to the girl.
(The Massena Observer., December 18, 1913, Page 1, Image 1)

YOUNGEST WOMAN PREACHER

Melesin K. Sowles, a girl of 16 years, is probably the youngest woman preacher in the world. In June of this year, **she preached the opening sermon in the yearly meeting of the Baptist Church, Haney Creek, WI; and she has been granted an unlimited license to preach at the quarterly meeting of that church.** Miss Sowles' home is at Prospect, WI, where her father is in charge of the Baptist Church. Miss Sowles has frequently, during the summer, spoken from her father's pulpit. **Before she was 10 years old, she evinced a great interest in theology and, unaided, outlined a sermon.**
(**Bolivar Breeze., May 10, 1900, Page 3, Image 3**)

GIRL PREACHER TALKS AT
NORTH END MISSION

A 16-year-old girl is preaching at the North End Mission this week. **Cloa Brooks**, a Richmond girl, gave an excellent sermon at the Mission last night and will preach each evening this week including next Sunday.

Miss Brooks, after her High School training, went to Westfield Bible Seminary in Westfield, and now has a regular charge in Monroe, at the Friends Church. She hopes to take more theological training later, and with her experience, she will probably be quite successful as a preacher.
(**The Richmond Palladium and Sun-telegram., April 30, 1917, HOME EDITION, PAGE FOURTEEN, Image 14**)

CHAPTER 5

AGED LADY PREACHERS

REV. LYDIA SEXTON

She Lives in Seattle, WA, and Is the Oldest Woman Preacher (Special Correspondence)

SEATTLE, WA

March 17—**Rev. Lydia Sexton**, of this place, is considered the oldest woman preacher in the United States. She was born on April 12, 1799, in Sussex County, now Rockport, NJ, and has been preaching for nearly fifty years of the ninety-three that she has lived....

Mrs. Sexton was the daughter of Rev. Thomas Casad, a Baptist clergyman. Lydia found herself an orphan when she was nine years old, and four years later, she left her home for the "far west," the "Hios," as Ohio was then called. The trip was a perilous one of 800 miles over the Alleghany Mountains and through an unsettled wilderness without roads or bridges and infested with bears and wolves and roving bands of Indians. She grew to womanhood in Ohio, and learned the glove making and tailoring trades. When quite a young woman, she married Isaac Cox, who accidently met death soon after the wedding day. In April 1824, she married Moses Moore, but he also died within a short time. On September 12, 1829, she married Joseph Sexton at Jacksonborough, OH, and with him she lived for over fifty years until his death.

In 1834, after a life of doubt upon religious matters, she joined the United Brethren Church and was baptized in the Great Miami River in Dayton, OH. A few days after joining the church, she went to a dance, being very fond of the amusement. When she entered the hall, she was suddenly stricken with a deep sense of disapproval of her own past conduct, and then she felt a call to teach the Word. She left the hall, deeply moved with the determination to become a minister. The opposition of her family, however, deterred her from carrying out her plans for several years, and it was not until eight or ten years later that she commenced to exhort in public. From the first, her success was notable.

In 1851, Josiah Turrell, presiding elder at the quarterly Illinois Conference of the United Brethren, gave her a license to preach, which license she still proudly exhibits. **Her forte was in revival work, and her converts during the twenty to thirty years following her regular initiation into the ministry numbered many thousands.**

In 1870, Mrs. Sexton, with her husband, moved to Kansas. She was no sooner there than she was importuned to preach. It seemed as if half the people of the state knew good old Mother Sexton; for many of the citizens of the new state had emigrated from Ohio, Indiana, and Illinois. Before she had fairly gotten to work, however, Governor Harvey appointed her prison chaplain at the state penitentiary. She took the position with some reluctance, for she was afraid she would not be able to successfully carry on the difficult duties. **She was over seventy years old, and her kind, motherly, and sympathetic tenderness awoke in many a poor man's breast the love he had borne for his own mother years before. When her labors there were finished, she counted ninety-nine converts among the jail birds who had embraced the Christian faith.** She went as a delegate in 1870 to the national prison congress at Cincinnati and was the only woman who addressed that distinguished body.

A year or two later, when the people of Kansas were in distress owing to several successive crop failures, she started out to solicit aid. Her appeals through the eastern states were rewarded by bountiful gifts of food and clothing, and at one time, she sent back a whole trainload of flour. Her good work was cut short by the receipt, while in Washington City, of a dispatch from the Governor of St. John, telling her not to send any further supplies, as the distress had been relieved.

About three years ago, Mrs. Sexton moved to Seattle from Kansas, and she still frequently preaches and makes trips to surrounding towns and hold revivals. During the past few weeks, her eyesight has gradually failed, and this will probably deter her from doing much more active work in the way of preaching.

She remembers the war of 1812 distinctly. Her brother, Abner, was in the war, and her grandfather on her mother's side, Joseph Tingley, and his two sons, were soldiers under Washington in the Revolution. She still remembers hearing her grandfather tell of his first meeting with General Washington. The old man, with his two sons, approached the General with some trepidation. Taking off his hat and putting it under his arm, he said:

"I believe I have the honor of being in the presence of General Washington!"

"My name is George Washington," replied the great man. "Put on your hat, Daddy."

"I came to offer you my services," said the old man, "and that of my sons, such as it is, to help in this struggle."

"Noble offering," said Washington. "Fall in ranks there, and at roll call report your names."

Mrs. Sexton says that she is going to live to be a hundred years old, and it is not at all unlikely that she will.
ELDEN W. POLLOCK
(**St. Lawrence Republican and Ogdensburg Weekly Journal., March 30, 1892, Page 7, Image 7**)

The oldest woman preacher in this country is the Rev. Lydia Sexton, who was born in New Jersey in 1799, and who still preaches in various parts of the west. **She predicts that she will live until 1900, thus extending her life into three centuries.** Mrs. Sexton is granddaughter of Marquis Anthony Cozot, who came to America early in the seventeenth century. She has many relations in New Jersey, Indiana, Ohio, Illinois, Kansas, Missouri, Arkansas, and Washington. Her memory is excellent and her sight remarkably good. Her voice is clear and melodious, and she delights to sing sacred songs to the congregation.
(**Watertown Times., June 20, 1891, Page 4, Image 4**)

The oldest woman in the country who is a preacher, it is thought, is the Rev. Lydia Sexton, of Seattle, now ninety-three years of age. She has been in service about half a century. For eight or ten years, she was an exhorter before receiving a regular license to preach in 1851.
(**South Side Observer., January 13, 1893, Page 4, Image 4**)

THE OLDEST WOMAN PREACHER

"Aunt" Penelope Gardiner recently died in Hesper, KS. She was ordained a minister in 1853, when she was thirty-three years old, and was a preacher up until her death. **She is said to have had the longest record as a preacher of any woman in this country.**

(The Sun., April 23, 1903, Page 4, Image 4)

—————

WOMAN PREACHER 107 YEARS OLD

The **oldest woman preacher** in the United States is Mrs. Mary Goddard of Brunswick, ME. **Mrs. Goddard, though 107 years old, continues to preach occasionally to congregations of Friends.**

(The Gilboa Monitor., January 03, 1918, Page 3, Image 3)

CHAPTER 6

FAMOUS WOMEN: HEALING EVANGELISTS OF YESTERYEAR

There are two well-known healing evangelists—Aimee Semple McPherson and Maria Woodworth-Etter—who God used powerfully despite many challenges in their personal lives as well as from people who did not believe that women should be in ministry. As you will see from the following newspaper clippings, thousands of lives were impacted for eternity as a result of their obedience to walk in their callings and fulfill their calls.

5,000 Are Baptized

That was the number won over by Aimee Semple McPherson, evangelist and faith healer, at meetings in St. Louis. Photo shows a convert being immersed.

LET WOMEN RIGHT EVE'S WRONG, SAYS WOMAN "BILLY SUNDAY"

"Woman brought sin into the world, didn't she? Then surely she should have the right to help undo the wrong and lead the world to the Eden above."

That is the answer of **Mrs. Aimee Semple McPherson**, the pretty 28-year-old Los Angeles **woman preacher** who is speaking nightly to enormous audiences of New Yorkers in her evangelistic campaign. Mrs. McPherson is an ordained minister of the **Apostolic Church**. I asked her to tell why she thinks a woman should have the right to preach the Gospel.

"Woman's personality, her tender sympathies, her simple, direct message—the woman-mother heart, brooding over the world, yearning to help its wayward sons and daughters—these are all qualities in favor of her right to tell the story of God's love," she replied.

"Women were co-laborers with Peter and Paul in their work. But did not the apostle say, 'Let your women keep silence in the churches?' Yes, but he did not refer to a Godly woman's right to preach the eternal Gospel, for he also gives specific instructions as to how a woman should conduct herself when preaching or praying in public. Before I consecrated my life to this service of love for God and humanity, I was an elocutionist. No one questioned my right to amuse the church congregation with witticisms and comical recitations. That was 'speaking in the church,' wasn't it?

"The best reason in favor of a woman's right to preach the Gospel is that God's favor has attended it, and blessed results follow. Called into work at 17, I have been in active service practically ever since. I have seen thousands come to the altar, laden with iniquity, then rising to their feet changed men and women."

(Bisbee Daily Review., September 03, 1919, Page 6, Image 6)

MIRACLE WORKER HANDS OVER HANDKERCHIEFS TO HEAL CRIPPLED AND SICK

The "Miracle Woman," Mrs. Aimee Semple McPherson, Canadian evangelist, preaching and conducting "healing services" in the McKendree Methodist Episcopal Church, continued today to aid the sick and the crippled through prayer. Word of sudden recoveries from illness and many healings have reached the church rectory.

Simultaneous with the announcement that Mrs. McPherson preaches her last sermon in Washington Sunday night, comes word from the Rt. Rev. Alfred Harding, Bishop of the Episcopal Diocese of Washington, that James Moore Hickson, a lay member of the Church of England, known as the "Miracle Man," will conduct "spiritual healing meetings" in the Trinity Church, Third and C Streets Northwest, on April 20, 21, and 22.

Both Mrs. McPherson and Mr. Hickson have stirred all *of* America with their miraculous healings through prayer.

LAME DISCARD BRACES

Mrs. McPherson conducted a healing service last Thursday which resulted in many cures. A lame man walked, a crippled boy removed his braces, a paralyzed boy ran for the first time in ten years, a colored woman moved her paralyzed arms and legs freely, a twelve-year-old girl regained the use of a paralyzed arm, and many recoveries from sickness resulted.

All day yesterday, men, women, and children visited the McKendree Church rectory in an effort to see the "Miracle Woman" and have her pray for them or for relatives who were afflicted. The telephone dinged every few minutes with requests that Mrs. McPherson make visits to the sick and crippled.

The "Miracle Woman" has been unable to *see* visitors or answer calls to visit homes. She, however, urges afflicted persons to send or bring a handkerchief, or some piece of cloth, to the church and tells them they will be prayed over and anointed. The handkerchief is then applied to the afflicted parts: Mrs. McPherson assures the afflicted that with faith in God they can be cured and urges them to send some piece of cloth to the church.

HEALED THROUGH HANDKERCHIEF

It was through the use of a handkerchief that Mrs. W. J. Jackson, of Baltimore, declared she was healed. She had one prayed over and anointed with oil and then applied to her back. In several weeks, she had entirely recovered from tuberculosis, after physicians had given up all hope for her recovery.

Since Mrs. McPherson's announcement regarding handkerchiefs, more than 100 of them have been received and prayed over. Rev. Charles A. Shreve, pastor of the church, said today he was sending more than fifty handkerchiefs to homes of persons sick or crippled.

Bishop Harding's announcement comes at a time when there is great interest being manifested in spiritual healings, and the "Miracle Man" from England is expected to perform many healings in this city. Preparations for accommodating a large number of afflicted are now being made at the Trinity Church.
(The Washington Times., April 10, 1920, Image 12)

MIRACLE EVANGELIST
AT WICHITA IN MAY

Dates for the great evangelistic and healing meetings by **Mrs. Aimee Semple McPherson** of Los Angeles, California, have been set for May 7 to 28, inclusive; and meetings will be held at the Forum.

Mrs. McPherson is 31 years of age and has conducted meetings throughout the United States, at which she prays for the sick. **Many hundreds and perhaps thousands have been healed of any and all so-called incurable diseases, by the power of God**, through Mrs. McPherson's earnest prayers and their own faith.

It seems to be impossible to find anywhere, a building that will hold the throngs that go to hear this woman of God, and Wichita expects to be filled to capacity during her stay there.
(The Liberal Democrat., April 27, 1922, Image 7)

WAS IT A MIRACLE?

AN AGED CRIPPLE WALKS AT THE
COMMAND OF AN EVANGELIST

ANDERSON, TN

Jan. 1—**Mrs. Maria B. Woodworth**... is conducting one of her characteristic revivals at the **Church of God**, in this city, which she founded three years ago. Monday evening, Mrs. Hiram Baxter, an aged lady of this city, hobbled to the church on crutches, having been unable to walk without them for two years, owing to rheumatism and to the effects of a fall.

She immediately kneeled at the altar and began a most fervent prayer in her own behalf, in which Mrs. Woodworth joined her. At the end of a half hour's prayer, Mrs. Woodworth, in a loud tone of voice, said: "In the name of Jesus of Nazareth, arise and walk!" whereupon the old cripple sprang to her feet and leaped over the railing at the altar, and shouted and sang from one end of the church to the other, and walked to her home, a half mile away, leaving her crutches at the church. Crowds of people gather at the church at every meeting.

(Daily Tobacco Leaf-Chronicle,. January 1, 1891, Page 1)

A MIRACLE WORKER

Alleged Remarkable Cures...

Mrs. Maria B. Woodworth Says Only a Recording Angel Can Properly Describe Her Work
"Diseases Given to Jesus"
Decatur (IL) Cor. Chicago Tribune

Mrs. Maria B Woodworth... who performs miracles and has created such a sensation in Indiana and Southern Illinois, has been at this city since Monday last, **closes her first six days' work here with a record of about thirty-five miracles performed and about one hundred souls saved**. In the midst of such excitement as we have here, the stories of Mrs. Woodworth's work are apt to grow by repetition, people unconsciously exaggerating the reports of her wondrous cures, so that there is some little difficulty in getting the exact facts. Mrs. Woodworth makes the blind to see, the deaf to hear, the lame to walk, the diseased to be made whole, and the sciatic and *rheumatic to jump for joy and glorify the Lord. She has cured* cancer, heart disease, brain trouble, epilepsy, consumption, catarrh, cuticura, in growing toenails, spinal disease, neuralgia, paralysis, boils, and a host of other diseases that flesh is heir to.

But one cannot believe all that is told of her. For instance, there is a little boy here who lost some of his toes by a freight train, and they tell it that Mrs. Woodworth touched the stump and new toes sprouted out. Mrs. Woodworth was asked about this case today and frankly acknowledged that it was not true. She said that it was the invention of a local reporter who is possessed of Satan.

In order to get at the facts of the case, the *Tribune* reporter spent all day with Mrs. Woodworth investigating her work. The sensation she has created and is creating is without parallel. She has been in the evangelizing business for the last six years, but until a comparative recent date, most of her work has been done in the vicinity of her native home in Ohio. Then she strayed over into Southern Indiana, and now she is in Illinois.

She numbers her miracles by the hundreds and her conversions by the thousands. She claims in brief to have been especially called by Jesus Christ to go out and heal the sick and preach the Gospel as did the apostles of old. She has frequent visions or trances during which she talks with the Savior and tastes of the joys of heaven; she is also sometimes given glimpses of the horrors of hell in order to spur her on to harder work in saving souls therefrom. She claims to be endowed with apostolic fire, or inspiration, the same as that given the Apostles on the day of Pentecost, when the Holy Spirit descended on them and they spoke with divers tongues. There is little doubt that Mrs. Woodworth is the coming evangelist. Mr. Moody is getting somewhat passé as an evangelist if one may use such a term—at least he needs a rest. Sam Jones has had his day; he needs a rest also. So do the people he has preached to. Harrison, the boy preacher, is now getting along toward sixty, and it is well enough to give him a rest. Mrs. Woodworth has the eloquence of Sam Jones, without his coarseness; she has the earnestness of Harrison with something more added; moreover, she is able to perform miracles, which is more than the others could do. Sam Jones claimed to have performed a miracle when he filled the Casino rink in Chicago chock full of people every night, and those who know Mr. Jones best are the readiest to acknowledge his claim. But that isn't the sort of miracle Mrs. Woodworth performs. **Hers are orthodox miracles of the Bible pattern. So far as the meager records in the case go, it would seem that she has already performed more miracles than all the apostles combined.**

The meetings here are held in Oakland Park, a pleasant picnic ground near the city limits. Mrs. Woodworth and her party of assistants are in a camp at the park, occupying six tents of their own. **She has also a large handsome, new tent, in which the meetings are held—a tent recently bought for her by some of her admirers and large enough to accommodate a seated audience of 1,500.** Her retinue is of a somewhat pretentious character. She has three comely young women with her—Miss Posther, Miss Isenberg, and Miss Daggett—who are living monuments of her power. **She saved one of them from blindness, another from a consumptives grave, and all three from the bottomless pit.** All three are good singers. They are also mighty in prayer. They are very energetic workers at the meetings. Miss Daggett also cooks for the party while the other two act as housekeepers or maids-in-waiting to Mrs. Woodworth. Mrs. Woodworth has also a business manager who attends to the advertising and sale of her books and photographs and who acts also as advance agent in making out the route. He is a shrewd young man, Mr. I. W. Dempsey, the business manager. Mrs. Woodworth has also a husband, Mr. P. H. Woodworth who acts as doorkeeper, assistant treasurer, and general factotum. These five form Mrs. Woodworth's regular and permanent staff, but in addition to these, she has a number of volunteer friends and camp followers who come along to shout and sing and testify and praise the Lord with tempestuous verbosity.

It will be noticed that the inquirer into Mrs. Woodworth's miraculous power has no trouble hunting up witnesses in her behalf. All are ready, nay, anxious, to tell what the Lord has done by the touch of Sister Woodworth's hands. Names and dates and references for proof of her marvelous work are thrust at one on all sides. There was Mrs. Turner of Warrensburg—eight miles from here—cured this week of heart disease; Mrs. Hanks of the same place cured of "rheumatism and disease of the lungs;" Jacob Major of Decatur cured of rheumatism and stomach troubles; Farmer Grover of Warrensburg cured of deafness and a pain in his back; Mrs. Harris of Urbana, Ill., cured of a very bad cancer; Mrs. Harriet Perkins of Urbana cured of female troubles of fifteen years standing, as certified to by Dr. White of New York and Dr. Miller of Urbana; Judge White of Anderson, Ind., cured of consumption; Father Sanders of Muncie, Ind., cured of consumption; Mrs. George Goodman of Decatur nearly cured of rheumatism; Miss Sage of Decatur cured of a frightful abscess on the bosom; Mrs. Buchert of Decatur nearly cured of paralysis—and so on and so on. There is no lack of witnesses.

The usual afternoon meeting, commencing at 2 p.m., was the first one attended by the *Tribune* reporter. **There were over 1,000 well-dressed people in the tent when the meeting began—somebody said it comprised the "bang-up elite" of Decatur.** The tent is circular, with a folding entrance like a circus tent. At the upper end, there is a raised platform about six feet wide by twenty feet long, and running at right angles from the center of this platform, there is another raised platform about twenty feet long by three feet wide. The whole structure is known as the altar, and its general shape is that of a capital T. Seated on the upper or main part of the platform were Mrs. Woodworth and her staff of assistants, professional and volunteer. No one sat near the elongation of the platform—the stem of the T, as it were—and it was seen later that this place was reserved for the sick, who were to come forward at a later stage of the proceedings and get cured.

The services from the start were marked by an intense fervor, a fact which was largely due to the energy of three young women assistants on the platform. The singing was most vociferous and in music, words, and method, very much like that heard at negro camp meetings at times of exceptional grace. The first song and the one that proved to be the favorite with Mrs. Woodworth's assistants, was one written by Mrs. Woodworth herself, the theme being the apostolic power with which she is endowed. It begins:

Tis the very same power
The very same power;
Tis the very same power
That they had at Pentecost;
Tis the power, the power;
Tis the power that Jesus promised should
come down

While with one accord assembled,
All in an upper room,
Came the power, etc.

With cloven tongues of fire
And a rushing mighty wind,
Came the power, etc.

Some thought they were fanatic
Or were drunken with new wine,
It was the power, etc.

Three thousand were converted
And were added to the church,
By the power, etc.

The martyrs had this power
As they triumphed in the flames, etc.

There seemed to be about fifty verses of this song, and the chorus was repeated until it seemed endless. Then there was prayer and then more singing—a great deal more.

Finally, Mrs. Woodworth began to preach, taking as her text:

"Behold I proceed to do a marvelous work, a marvel and a wonder in the midst of the people."

That is the sort of text she always uses, and she applies it directly to herself.

Mrs. Woodworth is a pleasant-faced lady, 42 years old, but looks younger, and is an easy, unembarrassed, and unpretentious speaker. She makes no preparation for her address—except by reading the Bible—she trusts to the inspiration of the Lord, she says—and she repeats herself considerably. In private conversation, she is quick witted, but the indications are numerous that her early education was somewhat neglected. She is rather above medium height and weight and has evidently a strong constitution, but she works so dreadfully hard in her services that her face bears many traces of fatigue and sleeplessness. Her blue eyes are weary and leaden until she begins to talk of her work, and then they flash with earnestness and an added color mounts her cheeks. She dresses plainly and neatly; today, she wore a plain navy blue woolen costume, with a roll of white tulle around her throat and a bunch of wild flowers in her bosom.

Her sermon was of the customary camp-meeting revival character. She spoke for about thirty minutes, marching up and down the platform hugging a large Bible to her bosom and occasionally smacking her hands together, and using other more or less excited and unique gestures. The moment she sat down, the young women vociferously began to sing. Then people were called on to testify. A man who said he had traveled eighty miles to be treated by Mrs. Woodworth, testified that he had heart disease for twelve years, "but had now given it to Jesus."

"And Jesus rebuked the disease and cast it out," said Mrs. Woodworth, with the air of one using a familiar quotation.

A woman got up and clapped her hands and looked up at the roof of the tent and said she saw the Saviour descending on her. Everybody shouted, "Amen!"

"Bless the Lord!" and so on, and away above the din of voices could be heard the voice of Miss Isenberg shouting:

"Sweet Jesus! Sweet Jesus!"

At this stage, the proceedings were comparatively quiet, the testifiers being given a chance to talk. The woman who was watching the roof of the tent was pulled into her seat, and a gray-haired, old man sprang up and said he had the "rheumatism bad, and the devil said he couldn't be healed."

"The old liar!" interrupted Miss Posther with loud indignation.

"Yes," continued the old man, "he's a liar, the biggest liar in two counties—I mean he's a-a-a liar."

The old man sat down at this point. A young woman sprang up and flung off her hat and began shouting incoherently, the tears flowing down her face.

"Oh, Jesus" shouted Miss Isenburg, "Sweet Jesus!"

Meantime the enthusiasm was rapidly increasing. Half a dozen people got up in rapid succession and told how they had given their diseases to Jesus. This was the phrase used in nearly every case, being the one employed by Mrs. Woodworth and her assistants Some of the diseases were very complicated, too, and a great many of them included "female troubles." The excitement grew until half a dozen or more people were on their feet together trying to testify, the girls on the platform egging them on loudly. Up to this point, Mrs. Woodworth had taken no very prominent part in this part of the exercises; presently she jumped up, ran rapidly down the altar platform as one runs down the springboard for a plunge into the sea, and shouted for those who wanted to be healed to come forward. The three girls also got off the platform, singing at the top of their voices. Seats were pulled forward for the sick so they could sit close up to the altar, and in a minute or two, there were at least twenty excited people seated there waiting to be cured.

Mrs. Woodworth has no general method of healing. Sometimes she does it one way, sometimes several others. The twenty sick people being seated at the altar, with their elbows or arms or faces resting on the same, Mrs. Woodworth walked all around them, hugging one and rubbing another, and whispering to a third, and kissing a fourth. She was manifestly in a state of great excitement, and the people she was performing on were no less so. The noise increased in fury, every moment. One had almost to yell at the top of his voice to make himself heard by the person beside him. Mrs. Woodworth got her arms around old Mrs. Buchert, who had been speechless and paralyzed for nine years, and hugged her and rubbed her bosom and face and shouted in her ears until the old woman got to her feet with the tears raining down her face and jumped up and down and jabbered inarticulately. Mrs. Woodworth yelled in her ear:

"Say 'Praise God.'"

She shouted this instruction over and over until the old woman evidently understood, and made most frightful attempts to speak the words she was commanded. It was said that she did speak some intelligible words and that her paralysis had nearly departed, but members of her family say that after she went home and calmed down she was nearly as bad as ever.

Mrs. Woodworth says it would take the recording angel to describe her meetings, so she doesn't expect that common reporters can do them justice. In fact, the frenzy and excitement were almost indescribable. The worst case, in one way, was Mike Phelan, a Roman Catholic. Mike has rheumatism and walks with a stick, and those three girls "lay for" everybody who has a stick. The reporter had one, but he held on to it. Mike limped to the front, and Mrs. Woodworth tackled him. She commanded him to straighten himself and put his foot down firmly, and the old man tried his best, but it was evidently a very painful task. Then she rubbed him vigorously, and as everybody knows Mike and watched the operation closely, Mike became somewhat embarrassed under the scrutiny.

"Drop your cane!" commanded Mrs. Woodworth.

Mike protested that he couldn't walk without his stick, but Mrs. Woodworth insisted that the Lord would support him. She caught the stick and pulled it from him, and one of the girls took it from her hands and threw it with a loud rattle on the platform Then the spectators who couldn't hear the conversation said to each other:

"Mike Phelan has thrown away his stick! And he is a Roman Catholic, too!"

For nobody ever saw Mike walking without the aid of a stick before.

"Walk and thank God!" shouted Mrs. Woodworth to Mike.

Mike tried it and squirmed.

I can't he said, "Gimme me shtick."

"Trust in the Lord. Have faith. Do without your stick until tomorrow at least," urged Mrs. Woodworth. "Give it a day's trial. Don't you feel better?"

"Yes ma'am, I do—but plaze gimme me shtick."

It looked as if Mike was sorry he came. Finally, he got his stick but walked with it under his arm until he was fairly out of sight. He said he was a good deal better.

Then the hysterical woman was helped to fix up her hair, the rheumatic were helped out to the street car, the sick and the well scattered, and the meeting adjourned.

At the evening meeting, there is a charge of 10 cents admission. Mr. Woodworth's photographs and books sell largely and bring in a goodly sum. The manager, Mr. Dempsey, was asked if the people who were healed paid a fee. He said nothing whatever was charged but acknowledged that voluntary offerings would be very welcome.

"But when they are cured," added Mr. Dempsey, "they mostly go off leaping and praising the Lord, and never think of money. Of course we cannot live on air."

All failures to heal are attributed by Mrs. Woodworth to a lack of faith on the part of the patients. The failures are therefore numerous. Mrs. Bradshaw, the wife of a Methodist preacher, was cured of paralysis, but had a relapse owing to lack of faith. Mike Phelan, it is reported tonight, has also a relapse and uses his stick just as before. The most miraculous cures were those of people who are not here. Mrs. Harris of Urbana was cured of a most frightful cancer.

It can be stated positively, however, that Mrs. Woodworth has performed many marvelous cures. Whether it is the force of will or of imagination or the intense excitement induced by her methods or the spirit of God acting supernaturally, she has certainly performed wonders in faith healing.

(Fort Worth Daily Gazette., October 08, 1887, Page 5, Image 5)

CHAPTER 7

LADY PREACHERS: FACTS, FANCIES, AND FUN

As you will see, the following are just random, fun, miscellaneous newspaper clippings.

A story is being told of a **woman preacher** who drew back the hymn book and said that she was going to throw it at the man who was untrue to his wife, and every man in the congregation dodged. This should not be accepted as an evidence of guilt. Probably every man in the congregation knew the unfailing inaccuracy of the woman's aim when she attempts to throw anything.—*Exchange*
(The Whitesville News., July 08, 1897, Page 2, Image 2)

A **lady preacher** married a couple lately in Iowa. At the end of the ceremony, the minister kissed the groom.
(The Meridional., July 27, 1889, Image 2)

NEWS AND NOTES FOR WOMEN

In the United States, lady doctors number 539; dentists, 420; while **68 are preachers**, and 20 practice as lawyers. Some ladies adopt two or three callings at once. A lady living in St. Louis notifies, on her door plate, that she is an elocutionist, poetess, washer, and ironer.
(The Long-Islander., May 07, 1880, Page 1, Image 1)

FACTS AND FANCIES

There are 275 lady preachers in the United States.
(The Brockport Republic., January 01, 1891, Page 4, Image 4)

In just 11 short years, within the United States, there were over 200 more women preachers.

A Cleveland lawyer has married a lady preacher. Perhaps he hopes she will be kept so busy getting up her Sunday sermons that he can escape.
(Cape Vincent Eagle., June 25, 1903, Page 2, Image 2)

NOT SATISFACTORY

"Our sexton doesn't like the new woman preacher."

"What are his objections?"

"He says she isn't strong enough to keep the dust pounded out of the pulpit cover."—*Chicago Record*
(The Watchman and Southron., January 19, 1898, Image 8)

SPURGEON REBUKED

Mr. Spurgeon was once traveling in a railway carriage. The only other occupant of which was a maiden lady of somewhat severe aspect; and to pass the time, he entered into conversation with her on various topics. The train happened to pass Kelvedon, in Essex, where Spurgeon first saw the light; and the preacher, who dearly loved a joke, pointed from the window and remarked: "A very great man was born there—Mr. Spurgeon, the eminent preacher." The lady looked at him with a stony stare for some time and then replied: "If St. Paul had been passing his birthplace, he would have said, 'A very great sinner was born there,' Mr. Spurgeon." It was the first intimation which the preacher had that he had been recognized by his traveling companion.

(Sistersville Daily Oil Review., October 25, 1904, Page 4)

CHAPTER 8

TO PREACH OR NOT TO PREACH?

THAT IS THE QUESTION!

For many centuries, there has been great debate about whether a woman should be allowed to preach; and, sadly, within some denominations this debate is still going on today.

SHALL WOMEN PREACH?

The question of licensing female preachers came up at the late session of the **Methodist Conference** at Sing Sing. The discussion grew out of the report made by one of the presiding elders, concerning the labors of a lady preacher in his district. At this point in the report, says the *Tribune*, the **Rev. Mr. Nichols rose and expressed his disapproval of any presiding elder's rising to submit to the conference the question of allowing female preachers. The Rev. Mr. McCanber moved that the conference disapprove of the practice of licensing women to preach.** The Rev. Mr. King moved that Mr. McCanber's motion be laid on the table, which motion was agreed to. **Some feeling was manifested during the discussion of the above motions, and one enthusiastic member wanted the conference to discuss fully the question of allowing female preachers. The lady alluded to is "widow Van Cott." She is the only licensed female preacher in the State of New**

York, and during the past winter has created an intense religious excitement wherever she has spoken. It is reported that she has converted nearly 2,000 persons during the past year. She is represented as being eloquent and very earnest. Some members of the conference are in favor of her continuing in the good work, while others are strongly opposed to it.

(The Evening Gazette., April 29, 1869, Page 4, Image 4)

RELIGIOUS INTELLIGENCE AND CHURCH ITEMS

...Rev. Theodore Cuyler is to be brought before the Presbytery of Brooklyn for inviting and permitting Miss Smiley, the well-known and eloquent lady preacher of the Society of Friends, to preach in his pulpit. Rev. Mr. Wheeler, of Poughkeepsie, permitted the same lady to occupy the pulpit of the **Presbyterian Church** there some weeks ago, and, therefore, is a subject for like discipline.

(The Catskill Recorder., February 16, 1872, Page 3, Image 3)

LADY PREACHING IN A CLERICAL COURT

On Monday next, February 5, at ten o'clock in the morning, the Presbytery of Brooklyn will meet in called session, in the First Presbyterian Church, on the corner of Fulton and Clinton Streets. The called session is to take action upon the report that the pastor of Lafayette Avenue Presbyterian Church, Rev. Theodore L. Cuyler, D. D., has recently invited and permitted a lady preacher, Miss Smiley, an orthodox Quaker minister, to occupy and preach in his pulpit. **The order of action of the Presbytery will be to hear a charge by testimony, and in either event, to pronounce such reprimand upon, or acquittal of, the clergyman as the facts of the case and the temper of Presbytery and the** constitution of the Church require or *Plattsburgh Republican.*, February 15, 1890, Page 2, Image 2 suggest. It is universally, though unofficially, known that Miss Smiley did preach in Lafayette Avenue Church as foresaid. That she did so with the foreknowledge and at the desire of the authorities of the church, is inferable from the preliminary advertisement of the event in this journal. It is well known that the allowance of woman-preaching is not only a contradiction to Presbyterian usage, but directly prohibited by Presbyterian fundamental law. Members of the Presbytery, however, regard the offense as more plain and technical than as any intended defiance of the Presbytery, and will adjudicate the matter more in the interest of relieving Presbytery from the impression of sanctioning such innovation—an impression that has gone abroad—than of personally arraigning Rev. Dr. Cuyler. That clergyman, however, will, of course, have an opportunity for, or defend, his action in the promises, to the Presbytery. The discussion of the event on which the indictment, to speak at large, is founded, has taken wide range in the correspondence column of *The Eagle*. Enthusiastic, gushing, and estimable men and women have taken the matter up on its intrinsic merits, and in its "progressive aspects." *The Eagle* will be imitated by the Presbytery when that body simply ascertains the facts and applies the written law thereto, without the intervention of personal, sympathetic, sentimental, or other irrelevant questions. That the deliberations and judgement of Presbytery will be correct and conducted in a spirit of charity, courage, calmness, and legality, the high character of the membership of that body and its recent demonstration of capacity for combing the severest technicality with the highest equity, area abundance evidence. The distinguished defendant himself has in his public writings, so often referred, directly or indirectly in critical or eulogistic terms, to his clerical colleagues in Brooklyn, that he is almost to be congratulated upon the opportunity and duty he has imposed upon them to constitute themselves a court on his case, limited, as they will be, by the prescriptions of exact law and not enjoying, like him, the wild freedom of journalistic essay-writing.

(The Brooklyn Daily Eagle., January 29, 1872, Page 2, Image 2)

LADY PREACHING

Miss Smiley, the lady preacher, has become the great sensation of today. She forces a direct decision on a question which frequently before, but never so pointedly, has challenged decision. **Miss Smiley appears to be gifted with exceptional talent for awakening religious interest in the hearts of the unrepentant. And this endowment, whether its subject be man or woman, is the truest ordination to the work of the ministry, as it is the special give of the Divine Father to his most favored children.**

But, we will be told, St. Paul says, "Let your women keep silence in the churches;" yet in a precious part of the same letter, he says, "every woman that prayeth or prophesieth with head uncovered dishonoreth her head." Now if she were not to pray or prophesy at all, why such stringent directions as to her costume? Neither can this refer to her private devotions, because it was in public that she was to be veiled. Paul doubtless intended women to keep silence in the churches, as a general rule, but if any woman by special endowment could pray or prophecy to edification she might do so, if she covered her head. And just here we remark, Miss Smiley wears a cap.

Woman does not keep silence in the church when she sings any more than when she prays. If a woman chants the Lord's Prayer, does she not take an active part in the worship of God as though she uttered the words without music? True, she does not speak, nor does she stand in the pulpit, but "Come unto Me all ye that labor and are heavy laden, and I will give you rest," beautifully sung, may be as persuasive an agent to bring souls to the Master as the preaching of a sermon from the same words.

It was written by the prophet Joel, "Your sons and your daughters shall prophecy," and the four daughters of Philip (Acts 21) are considered as proof of the fulfillment of the prediction as far as women are concerned. To prophesy does not, of course, always mean to teach; but it may mean that as well when it relates to women's work, as when it has reference only to that of a man.

It was *at* the sepulcher of the risen Saviour that women received, from the Divine Master himself, her commission to preach. He bade them go and proclaim the fact of his resurrection. The church was then only an assemblage of disciples, and all the preaching there was to do on the subject was to announce, "The Lord is risen!" and women were directed by the Risen Savior himself to perform this mission.
(Rockland County Journal., February 03, 1872, Page 4)

WOMEN AS MINISTERS

The opinion was recently expressed by a leading authority of the **Methodist Church** that women preachers will in time fill the majority of pulpits in the rural districts. Such a development would astonish some of the old timers who felt that women should keep silence in public places. But with women proving effective as political campaigners, there seems no reason why women should not also hold the attention of church congregations.

It might be objected that a woman preacher would not draw men. But perhaps the sight of a pleasing woman face in the pulpit might win some of the higher minds of the male sex.

Anyway, considering the present cost of living, many rural churches have either got to raise their salaries, or they will drive men with families out of their pulpits.

(News-dispatch., December 20, 1923, Page 6, Image 6)

HAMLIN PASTOR PROTESTS

The Rev. Paul Succop of Hamlin joined forces at the annual meeting of the **Eastern Lutheran Synod** held at Baltimore, MD, demanding that Mrs. Julius F. Seebach, wife of the pastor of the Luther Memorial Church, Philadelphia, stop preaching in her husband's pulpit during his visit to Europe.

The Philadelphia congregation also joined in protests, but the question of ousting the volunteer woman preacher from her husband's pulpit could not be considered at the meeting. Despite the storm of disapproval, Mrs. Seebach is reported to have declared she would preach every Sunday until her husband returns from Europe.—*Rochester Times-Union*

(The Hilton Record., July 09, 1925, Page 1, Image 1)

METHODISTS TO LICENSE WOMEN AS PREACHERS

Fifteen Already Granted Right to Appear in Pulpit
(By *The Associated Press*)

CHICAGO

Nov. 19—Fifteen women have been licensed as preachers in the **Methodist Episcopal Church** since this right was granted last May by the General Conference of the Church. Miss M. Madeline Southard reported here. Miss Southard is president of an association of women preachers here in the United States and

Canada that represents 15 denominations. She is director of evangelism of the Epworth League.

"The first woman preacher to be licensed in the Methodist Episcopal Church under this ruling," Miss Southard said, "was Miss D. Willia Caffrey of Wanatchee, WA. She came from a family of preachers and at the age of nine wanted to preach. She has been acting as associate pastor of the First Methodist Church at Wanatchee. Her pastor was at the General Conference, telegraphed word of its decision, and she was licensed by a local preacher within two hours.

At the time, she was 2,000 miles away in the east, but the enterprising Denverites called a meeting as soon as they heard the news and took action.

The first woman licensed in New England was Mrs. Kate Morrison Cooper. For the past three years, she had been pastor of the Methodist Episcopal Church at Portsmouth, RI. She was licensed June 10.

Ten days later, Miss Mabelle H. Whitney was licensed at Pittsfield, VT. She was a supply pastor and previously had served as pastor of a Congregational Church in Maine. Ten days after, Miss Capitola B. Lochnar was licensed by the Proctorsville, VT, M. E. Church; and in a week, another Vermont woman, Miss Ellen H. Wagner, a public school teacher, was licensed at Milton.

Miss Southard herself was the seventh woman preacher licensed.

"It is not an easy task to keep informed on how many women have been licensed," she said, "when they are being licensed right along in so many sections." "There is no doubt," Miss Southard added, "that ordination will be granted

Methodist women when the next General Conference meets in 1924."
(Plattsburgh Daily Press., November 20, 1920, Page 5, Image 5)

PRESBYTERIANS WILL HAVE GIRL PREACHER

CHICAGO

May 8—The action of the Chemung Presbytery, of Elmira, NY, in taking under its care **Miss Rachel G. Brooks**, a candidate for the ministry, will be declared unique in tomorrow's issue of the "Continent," a Presbyterian periodical. **It was only a year ago that the general assembly of the church voted ordination of women.**

Miss Brooks was graduated from Elmira College and wanted to preach in rural communities financially unable to support a regular pastor.
(The Columbia Herald., May 09, 1913, Page 6, Image 6)

BAPTIST polity gives that denomination trouble at times. That church has always opposed the ordination of women to the Gospel ministry. Yes the First Baptist Church of San Jose, California, has recently ordained Mrs. Aimee Semple McPherson. It seems that she has been a lay preacher in one of the small denominations and had gained some popularity as a preacher. Claiming that her views had changed to accord with those of the Baptists, she applied to that church for ordination, and she was ordained. The action of that church is final and there is no appeal from it. Although other Baptist Churches in the country may be opposed to this action, they can do nothing. Mrs. McPherson is an ordained Baptist minister.

(The Presbyterian of the South: [combining the] Southwestern Presbyterian, Central Presbyterian, Southern Presbyterian., August 30, 1922, Image 1)

CHAPTER 9

REVIVAL
AND
AWAKENING

THE 100-YEAR PROPHECIES

There are several 100-year prophecies from near the year 1900, which state that God is going to pour out His Spirit in a more powerful way than ever before and that we will see worldwide revival and awakening. Both Maria Woodworth-Etter and William Seymour prophesied about this coming end-time revival that will sweep across the face of this earth. I believe that we are in the birthing stages of this final outpouring of God's Glory upon Earth.

Many of the revivals that you read about in this book can help to spur us on in our faith to believe God that right now, He wants to do something extraordinary on this planet.

Pastor Michael Edds wrote the following article, and he gave us permission to share it with you in this book.

Great Spiritual Awakenings have swept the world over the centuries. They have changed lives and the very culture in which we live. An Awakening is a special time when God comes down and saturates a place and a people with His presence. There is a final Great Awakening coming.

The Final Great Awakening– An End-time Revival

The great Azusa Street Awakening, which over the years resulted in 600 million being swept into the Kingdom of God and gave birth to the Pentecostal Movement, began in 1906. It was one of the greatest outpourings of the Spirit of God since Pentecost. Multitudes were saved, healed, and filled with the Holy Spirit. Incredible miracles occurred.

This great revival moved from Los Angeles to its new focal point of Chicago, Illinois. The two great centers of revival in Chicago were the North Avenue Mission and the Stone Church. Pentecost swept from Chicago to Canada, Europe, South America, and Africa. One of the greatest outpourings occurred at Stone Church in 1913. The renowned evangelist Maria Woodworth-Etter began a revival on July 2, 1913 at Stone Church.

The services were to last until the end of July but continued for six months. This was a time of divine appointment for the city of Chicago; God rent the heavens and came down! Scenes from the days of the Early Church began to occur at Stone Church. Word began to spread throughout Chicago of miraculous healings, deliverance from demonic possession, conversions, and of the outpouring of the Holy Spirit happening in these meetings. Advertisement was no longer necessary! The city was incredibly shaken.

Word spread of the miraculous intervention of God. Thousands came on trolleys, buggies, and trains, while many walked. Some came from distances of 1,600 miles away. 1,200 to 1,500 packed into Stone Church each night. The basement was filled, and many stood out on the street. Street meetings were held to accommodate them. Three services were held on Sundays!

As Christians prayed around the altar one evening, Sister Woodworth-Etter and others gave the following powerful prophecy and divine promise, which they prophesied would occur within 100 years of the 1913 Chicago Visitation. She prophesied of this coming End Time Revival....

"We are not yet up to the fullness of the Former Rain and that when the Latter Rain comes, it will far exceed anything we have seen!"

Rev. William Seymour, the leader of the Azusa Street Awakening, also prophesied that **in 100 years there would be an outpouring of God's Spirit and His Shekinah Glory that would be greater and more far reaching than what was experienced at Azusa.**

It has been almost 100 years since these prophecies were given. In my own beloved church, I am seeing the beginnings of this prophecy being fulfilled.... Healing and miracles are occurring! The anointing of the Holy Spirit on the services is heavy and growing each week. Something IS happening! I believe that we have reached the time of the fulfillment of these 100-year-old prophecies. We must be diligent to pray, intercede, and protect what the Lord is doing. We must encourage and edify one another as never before. We must crucify every critical, judgmental, and religious spirit that may be within us. We must put on the holiness and righteousness of Christ. Our time of divine destiny has come. We are about to experience what Brother Seymour and Sister Woodworth-Etter foresaw. God is about to rend the heavens and come down! The greatest revival in the history of the church is at hand!

Be encouraged, God is on the Move in our generation!

In Closing

I pray that this book has been thought provoking and challenging for you and that it will expand your vision regarding women in ministry. Let's be open to allowing God to move—His way, in our day! There are many other things that I could have shared regarding women in ministry, but I believe that these are the things that God wants me to include in this book… **FOR SUCH A TIME AS THIS.**

May God bless you, prepare you, strengthen you, lead you, guide you, give you wisdom, and use you to help bring in the final harvest of souls in these last days in which we are living. This is an exciting time to be alive!

SALVATION PRAYER

If you don't already know Jesus as your Lord and Savior and you want to, please pray the following prayer from deep within your heart to enter into a relationship with Him:

Dear Jesus,
I admit that I am a sinner, and I need You. Thank you for dying on the cross in my place and taking my punishment. Please forgive me for my sins and come into my heart and be my Savior and my Lord. Please help me to live for You from this day forward. Thank you for making me part of Your family. In Jesus' Name, Amen.

If you prayed this prayer sincerely from your heart, you are now a child of God. You have just taken your first step in your journey with Him. Welcome to His family!

ACKNOWLEDGMENTS

POWERFUL WOMEN OF GOD IN MINISTRY TODAY

Reverend Cindylee Bohley – *Pastor and Teacher*
Jacob's Well Family Worship Center, Cambridge, NY
www.jacobswellfellowship.com/

Prophet Esther Emmons – *Prophet and Pastor*
Prophetic Destiny Ministry, Johnstown, NY
www.pdministry.org/

Donna Schambach – *Evangelist and Teacher*
Schambach Ministries International, Tyler, TX
www.schambachfoundation.org/

Reverend Sharon Miller – *Pastor and Revivalist*
Sinks Grove, WV

Nancy Insley – *Teacher*
His Healing Touch, OR
HisHealingTouchMinsitry@msn.com

Heather Bartos – *Worship Leader*
Cooperstown Assembly of God, Cooperstown, NY

Michelle Adams – *Worship Leader*
Rock Road Chapel, Berne, NY

Reverend Yong Brierly – *Pastor and Revivalist*
River of Destiny Church, Lostant, IL
www.riverofdestinychurch.com/

Reverend Tammi McVeigh – *Pastor and Worship Leader*
House of Grace, Bingen/White Salmon, WA
www.houseofgracewa.org/

Nicole Banta – *Missionary*
Granville, NY
www.thenicolebanta.wordpress.com/

Patti Dahl – *Evangelist and Gospel Singer/Songwriter*
Elder for the State of Connecticut for Gospel Ministerial Alliance
Patti Dahl of Heartsong, Naugatuck, CT
www.heartsongsingersforchrist.com/

PHOTOGRAPHERS

Robbie Batchelor – Thank you for generously providing the author's photo for the back cover of this book.

Cindy Cassidy – Thank you for sharing your beautiful photo for use on the front cover of this book.

Made in the USA
Middletown, DE
10 May 2022